Public Speaking Unlocked

Practical Steps to Manage Anxiety, Conquer your Fears, Build Confidence to Develop Engaging and Persuasive Communication Skills

By Patrick Edwards

TABLE OF CONTENTS

Introduction

It was a bright summer Sunday morning in 2010 in Birmingham, United Kingdom, around 11:15 a.m. I stood behind the pulpit, facing the congregation, ready to give my "preach with a view" audition to determine if I'd become the minister in charge of my chapel. My heart raced as I prepared to deliver my carefully crafted sermon. The familiar anxiety of public speaking loomed over me, a feeling I had struggled with throughout my life.

I noticed an anxious young woman in the front row as I spoke. This reminded me of my early experiences when public speaking felt like scaling an uncharted mountain. But as I continued, something shifted within me. The words started to flow, my nerves eased, and I saw her nodding in understanding. At that moment, I realised that overcoming the fear of public speaking isn't just about managing my nerves; it's about connecting with others and helping them find their voice. At the end of the presentation, many members gave me positive feedback, which encouraged me. The church later held a unanimous vote appointing me as their clergy.

My name is Patrick Edwards, and I have spent over two decades as a Reverend Minister. Speaking to different groups has been a massive part of my life, and while it hasn't always been easy, I have faced the same fears and doubts many experience. I preach to my parishioners at least three times a week and have spoken at various events—academic groups, conferences, weddings, funerals, and community gatherings. I understand your struggles, and my greatest desire is to help you conquer your fears and anxieties about public speaking so you can achieve your dreams.

In this book, I aim to provide practical steps and strategies to help you manage your anxiety, build your confidence, and improve your public speaking skills. We will explore common challenges many face, including fear of judgment and stage fright, which can make stepping onto the stage feel overwhelming. Organising your thoughts can be tricky and may lead to concerns about delivering a monotone speech or failing to connect with your audience. Recognising that these feelings are valid is essential; you are not alone in grappling with them.

This book offers a unique approach to overcoming public speaking challenges, combining practical strategies, personal stories, and engaging exercises that boost your confidence. Drawing from my experience, research, and inspiration from people like Leslie Brown, Jim Rohn, Zig Ziglar, Norman Vincent Peale, Tony Robbins, Andy Harrington, and many more who are great public speakers in our generation, I present actionable solutions that have helped many, including myself. You can trust the methods outlined in these pages to tackle your public speaking anxiety. With these insights, you will feel more prepared, engage your audience effectively, and elevate your confidence in every speaking situation.

You will learn how to structure your presentations, engage your audience, and communicate clearly and with confidence. You will also discover how to manage your time effectively and navigate technical challenges with ease.

Research shows that many struggle with public speaking anxiety. As you read this book, I invite you to join me on this journey of self-discovery. Together, we will confront your fears and uncover the courage within you, equipping you with the skills needed to transform your public speaking abilities.

Let's embark on this transformative journey together, setting the stage for the guidance and tools that await you in the upcoming chapters. Your involvement is essential as you read, think about your own experiences, and apply the strategies we discuss. This will be an active learning experience—a partnership. Together, we will conquer your public speaking fears and help you become the confident, engaging speaker you aspire to be.

Chapter 1:
Overcome Anxiety and Build Your Confidence

Have you ever felt your heart pounding, your palms sweating, and your stomach twisting in knots as you prepared to speak in front of a group? If so, you're not alone. That surge of adrenaline, that sudden wave of anxiety, is something many of us experience when faced with public speaking or high-pressure situations. But what if I told you that this feeling—this very sensation you might dread—could actually be a powerful tool rather than a crippling weakness?

I learned this lesson first hand one Sunday morning when I was scheduled to deliver a sermon to a packed congregation. As I waited for my turn to step up, I felt the familiar jitters creeping in. My hands felt clammy, my heart pounded relentlessly, and my mind raced with doubt. What if I forget my words? What if I lose my train of thought? What if I fail to connect with the audience?

For years, I had viewed this nervous energy as an enemy—something to be conquered or, at the very least, suppressed. But in that moment, I had a realisation: What if this energy wasn't something to fear but something to harness?

Instead of fighting the anxiety, I leaned into it. I took a deep breath and acknowledged what was happening inside me. My body wasn't betraying me; it was preparing me. The adrenaline coursing through my veins wasn't a signal of weakness but a natural response designed to heighten my senses, sharpen my focus, and give me the presence I needed to deliver my message with conviction.

And it worked. As I stepped up to speak, I didn't crumble under the pressure—I felt more alive than ever. My voice steadied, my words flowed naturally, and the energy I once feared became the very thing that fuelled my passion.

I encountered a similar challenge when I stood before an audience at an academic Conference at Bible College. The setting was different, but the feelings were the same—tightness in my chest, a sense of vulnerability, the overwhelming thought that I might not measure up. But again, I reminded myself: This energy is not my enemy. Instead of resisting it, I allowed it to drive me forward. I focused on my message, trusted in my preparation, and let that nervous energy propel me into a state of heightened awareness and engagement.

The difference was undeniable. Rather than letting anxiety shrink me, I let it expand me. I spoke with greater confidence, I connected more deeply with my audience, and I walked away from that experience with a profound new understanding: fear and excitement are two sides of the same coin. When we reframe our perspective, what once felt like an insurmountable obstacle can become one of our greatest strengths.

I share these experiences because I know how paralyzing anxiety can feel. It can make us doubt ourselves, hold us back, and keep us from stepping into opportunities meant for us. But the truth is, anxiety doesn't have to be the thing that stops you—it can be the thing that propels you forward. The key is in how we interpret it. When we stop seeing nervous energy as a threat and start seeing it as fuel, we gain access to a powerful force that can transform the way we show up in the world.

So the next time you feel those familiar jitters creeping in, don't fight them. Embrace them. Recognise them for what they are—a sign that you care, that you're stepping into something meaningful, that you're alive. And most importantly, remember this: your energy isn't your enemy. It's your greatest ally.

1.1 Embrace Nervous Energy

Anxiety before public speaking is often perceived as a significant barrier. However, what if we could change our perspective? The adrenaline running through your body can be transformed into a powerful asset to enhance your performance. This natural response prepares you for action, sharpening your focus and heightening your senses, ultimately giving you an advantage. Rather than viewing anxiety as an adversary, embrace it as a catalyst for excellent delivery. Use that energy to infuse your words with passion and conviction.

As you step up to the podium, harness that adrenaline to amplify your presence. It's not about eliminating anxiety completely but about redirecting it to work in your favour. Take inspiration from Winston Churchill, a master orator who recognised the profound impact of emotions in public speaking. Before delivering his speeches, Churchill engaged in rituals that transformed his nerves into impactful oratory. Despite the immense pressure, he skilfully used repetition and rhythm to connect with his audience's emotions, crafting speeches that inspired nations. His ability to turn anxiety into a dynamic stage presence exemplifies the potential we all have to transcend our fears and captivate those around us.

Finding the right rhythm and connection with your audience is essential for delivering an impactful message. To manage nervous energy, consider incorporating physical techniques before your speech.

Simple exercises, like jumping jacks (A full-body workout that involves jumping while spreading your legs and raising your arms) can help release excess adrenaline and ground you in the moment.

Power posing—standing tall with your feet apart and hands on your hips—can also boost your confidence and reduce stress. These minor adjustments can significantly enhance your approach to delivering your speech.

Reframing your thoughts about anxiety can be a transformative shift, allowing you to harness its energy rather than feel overwhelmed by it. Cognitive Behavioural Therapy (CBT) provides a range of practical techniques designed to help you reshape your mind-set, moving from a place of negativity and self-doubt to one of confidence and control. Instead of interpreting anxiety as a sign of failure or weakness, try viewing it as a natural response that signals you are prepared and ready to perform at your best.

This is where the power of positive thinking plays a crucial role. By acknowledging and redefining your physical sensations—such as a racing heart, sweaty palms, or shallow breathing—you can begin to see them not as indicators of fear or impending disaster but as evidence that your body is gearing up to help you succeed. These physiological responses are part of your body's way of sharpening focus, increasing alertness, and providing the energy needed to rise to the occasion.

Shifting your perspective in this way can have a profound impact on how you experience and manage anxiety. When you begin to see it as a source of motivation rather than distress, you take back control over your emotions and reactions. With practice, this mind-set shift can lead to greater resilience, improved performance, and a healthier relationship with anxiety in both personal and professional situations.

Interactive Exercise: Reflection Section

Think back to a recent speaking experience—perhaps a presentation at work, a speech at an event, or even a casual discussion where all eyes were on you. What physical sensations did you notice in your body? Did your heart start racing? Did your palms feel clammy, or did you sense a tightness in your chest? At that moment, how did you interpret these feelings? Were they signs of fear and impending failure, or simply your body's natural response to a high-stakes situation?

Now, consider a different perspective. What if those very sensations were not warnings of disaster, but signals of readiness? Your body is priming itself for success, sharpening your focus, and giving you the energy to engage fully. The next time you feel that surge of nervous energy, try to reframe it as excitement—an indication that you care about what you're about to say and that you're stepping up to a challenge.

Take a moment to write down your thoughts. How can you use this awareness to your advantage in the future? What specific strategies can help you transform nervousness into enthusiasm? Perhaps deep breathing exercises, power poses, or mental reframing techniques can help you harness this energy and turn it into a passionate, confident performance.

By reflecting on past experiences and planning ahead, you can develop a structured approach to managing nervous energy, ensuring that it fuels you rather than holds you back. Over time, this shift in mind-set can lead to greater confidence and a more empowering relationship with public speaking.

1.2 Breathing Techniques for Calmness

Understanding the power of controlled breathing can make a significant difference in public speaking. It's more than just a relaxation technique—it's a tool for regulating your nervous system, managing emotions, and projecting confidence. When faced with high-pressure situations, the body's natural response is often shallow, rapid breathing, which signals stress to the brain. This can heighten anxiety, making it difficult to think clearly and express yourself effectively. However, by intentionally practising controlled breathing, you can shift from a state of tension to one of calm, allowing you to speak with clarity and assurance.

Breathing deeply and intentionally activates the parasympathetic nervous system, which serves as the body's natural counterbalance to stress. This system slows the heart rate, lowers blood pressure, and promotes relaxation, helping to neutralise the fight-or-flight response that often accompanies public speaking. When you take control of your breath, you send a powerful message to your brain: I am safe. I am in control. This simple shift in awareness can greatly enhance your ability to focus and engage with your audience.

One of the most effective breathing techniques for managing nerves is diaphragmatic breathing, also known as belly breathing. Unlike shallow chest breathing, which creates tension and restricts airflow, diaphragmatic breathing allows for fuller, deeper breaths that calm the body and mind. This technique engages the diaphragm, the primary muscle responsible for respiration, and encourages slow, controlled breaths that enhance relaxation and focus.

To practice this technique, start by sitting or standing in a comfortable position with relaxed shoulders. Place one hand on your chest and the other on your abdomen. As you inhale deeply through your nose, let your abdomen expand while keeping your chest still.

Exhale slowly through your mouth, feeling your abdomen contract gently. Repeating this process several times can help train your body to respond to stress with composure rather than panic. Over time, diaphragmatic breathing becomes second nature, serving as a reliable anchor during high-pressure speaking engagements.

Breath control is not just a preparation tool—it can be used throughout a speech to maintain confidence and clarity. Taking a moment to engage in deep, rhythmic breathing before stepping on stage can help centre your mind and body. If anxiety arises mid-speech, pausing to reset your breath can restore a sense of control and enhance your delivery. These moments of grounding not only ease nerves but also improve speech cadence, making your presentation more engaging and impactful.

Mastering your breath means mastering your presence. Controlled breathing is not just about calming anxiety—it's about transforming nervous energy into a source of strength. The next time you prepare for a speaking engagement, remember that your breath is one of your greatest assets. By using it with intention, you can project confidence, connect with your audience, and turn nervousness into a powerful, commanding presence.

To practice diaphragmatic breathing effectively, start by sitting up straight with a relaxed posture. Drop your shoulders, ensuring there's no unnecessary tension in your upper body. Place one hand on your chest and the other on your abdomen. As you inhale deeply through your nose, focus on expanding your belly rather than your chest. This movement indicates that your diaphragm is actively working, pulling air into the lower part of your lungs where oxygen exchange is most efficient. As you exhale slowly through pursed lips, allow your belly to naturally flatten, releasing all the air in a controlled manner. By practicing this technique regularly, you can improve your breathing efficiency, enhance vocal control, and create a steady, confident rhythm in your speech. The ability to regulate airflow effectively not only improves clarity but also reduces strain on your voice, making your communication more powerful and engaging.

In addition to diaphragmatic breathing, several other techniques can help reduce anxiety and enhance focus before speaking. One highly effective method is the 4-7-8 breathing technique, which is simple yet powerful in calming the nervous system. To practice this, inhale quietly through your nose for a count of four, allowing your lungs to fill steadily. Hold your breath for a count of seven, giving your body time to absorb the oxygen fully. Then, exhale completely through your mouth for a count of eight, ensuring that all the air is released. This extended exhalation helps slow your heart rate, quiet your mind, and promote a deep sense of relaxation. This technique is particularly useful in high-stress situations, making it an excellent tool to use before stepping on stage or addressing an audience.

Another powerful breathing method is box breathing, which is widely used by athletes, military personnel, and professionals in high-stress environments. Often referred to as the 4-4-4-4 technique, this practice involves inhaling deeply for four counts, holding the breath for four counts, exhaling for four counts, and then holding again for four counts before repeating the cycle. This structured breathing pattern helps regulate your nervous system, reduce cortisol levels, and clear your mind, making it a valuable technique for maintaining composure in high-pressure speaking engagements. The rhythmic nature of box breathing makes it easy to implement anywhere, whether you're preparing backstage, sitting in a meeting, or simply trying to regain focus before speaking.

Integrating these breathing exercises into your daily routine can significantly improve your ability to manage stress and build resilience over time. One way to incorporate them is by starting your morning with a brief breathing session. Practicing diaphragmatic breathing upon waking can create a calm, centred mind-set that carries into the rest of your day. Another effective habit is to practice breathing techniques during your commute, whether you're driving, walking, or using public transportation. Box breathing can be synchronized with the rhythm of your steps or the hum of the engine, turning idle moments into opportunities for stress management. The more consistently you engage in these exercises, the more natural and automatic they will become, allowing you to draw upon them effortlessly when facing public speaking challenges.

By making controlled breathing an intentional part of your preparation and daily life, you cultivate a sense of inner steadiness that enhances both your confidence and presence. Instead of allowing anxiety to dictate your speaking experience, you can use breath control as a tool to transform nervous energy into clarity, composure, and impactful communication.

Many individuals who have used these techniques find them compelling. Yoga practitioners often highlight how vital breath control is for mental and physical health. Many have noticed a significant decrease in anxiety and an increase in focus and confidence from regular practice. Their experiences show that breathing is a basic need and a tool to help manage emotions. By using controlled breathing in your routine, you can take advantage of its calming effects, allowing you to face public speaking more confidently and efficiently.

1.3 The Power of Visualisation

Visualisation is like stepping onto a stage and feeling the warmth of the spotlight, knowing that every pair of eyes is focused on you, eagerly awaiting your words. For many, this moment may spark a surge of anxiety or nervousness—but it doesn't have to. Visualisation is a powerful and transformative technique that allows you to mentally prepare for success, helping you shift your focus from fear to confidence before you even speak a word.

Athletes have long understood the value of this practice. In the world of sports psychology, visualisation is used to enhance performance by creating vivid mental images of success. Whether it's the precise arc of a tennis serve or the rhythm of a perfect dive, athletes mentally rehearse the details to sharpen their focus and calm their nerves. The same technique can be applied to public speaking. By imagining yourself delivering a clear, confident speech, you can build mental and emotional readiness, reduce anxiety, and enhance your overall performance.

To begin, find a quiet space where you can concentrate without interruption. Close your eyes and picture yourself standing tall and composed, your voice strong and steady. Imagine the audience leaning in, nodding, smiling—fully engaged in your message. This mental rehearsal allows you to 'experience' a successful outcome in advance, giving your mind a template of what confidence feels like under pressure.

An important part of visualisation is rehearsing your connection with the audience. Picture yourself making eye contact, pausing at the right moments, using gestures naturally. Anticipate questions and visualise yourself responding with clarity and calm. This kind of mental preparation is particularly helpful in reducing the fear of the unknown—something that often fuels pre-speech anxiety.

To deepen the effect, create a visualisation script that maps out each stage of your presentation. Include sensory details: the warmth of the stage lights on your skin, the sound of your voice echoing confidently, the rustle of your notes or the softness of the microphone. Start with your opening line and carry the mental image all the way through to the final applause. The more vividly you engage your senses, the more real—and achievable—the experience becomes.

Scientific research supports the impact of visualisation. Studies suggest it can influence the brain's structure, strengthening neural pathways linked to confidence and calm. By regularly envisioning successful outcomes, you begin to train your brain to associate public speaking with achievement rather than fear. These mental rehearsals help make success feel not only possible but familiar.

Consider a seasoned speaker preparing for a keynote address. Long before they step onto the stage, they've already 'seen' it: the opening smile, the audience's response, the moments of connection and persuasion. They've mentally rehearsed tricky sections and anticipated questions. This preparation reduces uncertainty, enhances performance, and allows them to remain composed, even under pressure.

Incorporating visualisation into your public speaking routine isn't just about calming nerves—it's about laying the groundwork for real, repeatable success. When you train your mind to expect confidence, clarity, and connection, you give yourself the best chance of achieving just that. Over time, what was once a source of stress becomes an opportunity to shine.

1.4 Mindfulness Practices for Speakers

In an increasingly chaotic world, mindfulness offers a powerful means of finding calm and clarity. At its heart, mindfulness is the practice of being fully present—aware of your surroundings, thoughts, and actions—without becoming overwhelmed by external pressures or internal distractions. This quality becomes particularly valuable in high-stress situations like public speaking. Rather than spiralling into worries about potential mishaps or obsessing over audience reactions, mindfulness helps anchor you in the present moment, allowing for more confident engagement and meaningful connection with your listeners.

Incorporating mindfulness into your daily routine lays the groundwork for resilience against anxiety. It nurtures mental clarity, emotional steadiness, and a stronger sense of self-awareness. One effective technique is the body scan meditation: slowly and deliberately bringing your attention to each part of your body, from head to toe, noticing areas of tension and consciously releasing them. This simple yet powerful practice helps ground you in your body, calming the mind and easing physical stress—ideal preparation for the demands of public speaking.

Another technique is mindful listening—tuning into the ambient sounds around you, whether it's birdsong, the rustle of leaves, or the distant hum of traffic. This form of presence pulls you out of a busy mind and into the here and now, helping cultivate a peaceful mental state that can be carried into the spotlight.

When preparing to speak, short, targeted mindfulness exercises offer immediate relief from nerves. Grounding techniques, such as noticing the feeling of your feet on the floor or the texture of your clothing, help redirect your focus to your physical experience. Mindful breathing, where you pay close attention to the rhythm of your inhale and exhale, can slow your heart rate and quiet your thoughts—setting the tone for calm, clear, and confident communication.

Scientific research continues to highlight the lasting benefits of mindfulness for confidence and composure. Numerous studies have shown that regular mindfulness practice significantly reduces anxiety while improving self-assurance. In one longitudinal study, participants who maintained a mindfulness practice over several months reported notable improvements in their confidence levels and a marked reduction in stress. These findings suggest that mindfulness doesn't just offer temporary relief—it can fundamentally reshape how we respond to pressure, enabling a more composed and focused mind-set when speaking in public.

Mindfulness also enhances the way we connect with our audience. By treating each listener as though you are speaking directly to them, you foster a sense of personal connection and trust. This approach makes your message more relatable and impactful. Being fully present allows you to read the room more intuitively, respond to feedback in real time, and adjust your delivery in ways that resonate with your audience. The result is a speech that feels authentic, grounded, and emotionally engaging.

Ultimately, mindfulness does more than soothe nerves—it transforms how we experience public speaking. What once felt like a source of fear becomes an opportunity for connection, growth, and mutual understanding. Embracing mindfulness allows us to step onto the stage with clarity and purpose, knowing that we're equipped not only to speak, but to truly *connect*.

As we move forward, carry these mindfulness practices with you— not just for your next presentation, but in all areas of life. Approach each speaking opportunity with presence, curiosity, and the intention to engage deeply. In the next chapter, we'll explore how to craft your speech with structure and style—ensuring your message is not only heard, but remembered.

Chapter 2:
How to Master Speech Structure

2.1 The Power of a Strong Opening in Speech

In the last chapter, we uncovered the secret to captivating an audience from the very first moment—the power of a strong opening. But behind every confident delivery, there's often a quieter, more personal story unfolding: the inner tension, the self-doubt, the racing thoughts. These feelings can creep in just seconds before you speak, making your mind feel foggy and your message feel distant.

Before a speaker can command the room, they must first confront what's happening inside. Anxiety is one of the most common barriers in public speaking, but it doesn't have to hold you back. In fact, that nervous energy can be transformed into fuel—if you know how to manage it.

As a speaker steps onto the stage, there's an immediate surge of energy that fills the room, drawing the audience in with their resonant voice and compelling words. But what makes those initial moments so striking? It's all about the power of a strong opening. An engaging start is essential in public speaking; it sets the tone for what's to come, creates lasting first impressions, and ultimately determines whether the audience leans in with curiosity or drifts off into distraction.

Those first words can be your most valuable tool as you prepare to speak. They are your opportunity to build credibility and make an immediate connection with your listeners. A captivating opening isn't just a nice touch—it's the key to unlocking your audience's attention and inviting them into your message. Without an impactful beginning, even the most important ideas risk being lost.

To make those opening moments count, think of it as a dialogue, not just a monologue. A strong start should resonate with the audience, surprise them, and seamlessly connect to the themes of your speech. You might start with a quote that perfectly aligns with your main idea, drawing the audience into a shared understanding. A thought-provoking question can also spark curiosity, challenging the audience's assumptions and encouraging them to engage right from the outset. When executed well, these techniques elevate your speech from ordinary to extraordinary.

One of the most effective ways to craft an engaging opening is through storytelling. A well-told story captures attention and helps your audience connect with you on a personal level. Think of a meaningful moment from your life that ties directly to your message. Sharing a personal story not only makes you more relatable as a speaker, but it also fosters an emotional bond with your listeners. They see themselves in your experiences, recognise shared struggles or triumphs, and become more open to your ideas. The true power of storytelling lies in its ability to break down barriers and speak directly to universal human emotions. By sharing your journey, you invite your audience to join you in exploring deeper themes, sparking empathy and understanding.

Consider some of the most memorable openings in public speaking, which had a profound impact on audiences worldwide. Martin Luther King Jr.'s iconic "I Have a Dream" speech begins with a stirring call to action that immediately engages the crowd. His words tell a story of hope, change, and the vision for a better future, setting the tone for a message that would reverberate for generations.

Similarly, President John F. Kennedy's inaugural address on January 20, 1961, opens with a call for unity, challenging Americans to ask what they can do for their country. These speeches are more than just words; they are invitations to join in a collective purpose, resonating deeply with listeners and inspiring action.

A powerful opening creates momentum and a sense of anticipation. It primes your audience to listen attentively, not just because they must, but because they want to. By using strong, engaging openings, you can ensure that your message not only reaches your listeners but also leaves a lasting impact that stays with them long after your speech is over.

Interactive Exercise: Craft Your Opening with Strength

1.   Take a moment to draft the opening of your speech or presentation.

2.   Start by identifying the central message you want to share.

3.   Consider using a powerful quote, a thought-provoking question, or a personal story to engage your audience from the beginning.

4.   Write your opening with a focus on clarity and connection. Once you have a draft, read it aloud to yourself or a friend.

5.   Please pay attention to its emotional impact and look for ways to improve.

This exercise will help you create engaging and memorable openings, setting the stage for a successful speech.

Remember, your opening is your chance to grab attention, establish the tone, and connect with your audience; whether it's a quote, question, or story, a strong beginning can make all the difference in leaving a lasting impression.

2.2 Develop a Captivating Narrative

A speech built solely on facts may inform, but it rarely inspires. To truly captivate an audience, structure your speech like a story. Storytelling transforms your message into a shared experience—one that evokes emotion, stirs curiosity, and invites listeners on a journey they can follow and feel part of.

At the heart of any compelling narrative are three key elements: characters, conflict, and resolution. Introducing characters your audience can relate to gives them someone to root for. The challenges these characters' face creates tension and interest, while their triumphs offer closure and satisfaction. This narrative arc keeps your listeners engaged and allows your message to land with greater depth and meaning.

Emotional connection is essential if you want your message to leave a lasting impression. Emotional hooks—moments in your story that awaken empathy, curiosity, or hope—help forge that connection. Sharing personal stories of hardship, perseverance, or success invites your audience to relate to you, and more importantly, to see their own struggles and aspirations reflected in your journey.

For instance, I often share with my parishioners the financial challenges I endured as a young boy in Africa, and how I overcame them with faith and resilience. These moments of vulnerability and gratitude turn my message from a lecture into a conversation—one where the audience feels seen, understood, and inspired.

Such emotional engagement doesn't just amplify the impact of your speech; it ensures your message remains with your audience long after the applause fades. It fosters a sense of shared humanity, which is the bedrock of effective communication.

Incorporating personal anecdotes and case studies adds another layer of richness to your speech. Personal stories bring authenticity, helping to ground abstract ideas in lived experience. They demonstrate that what you're saying is not only possible—it's real. Meanwhile, case studies offer evidence to support your message, lending it weight and credibility. Used together, these elements help your audience both feel and believe in what you're saying.

However, emotional resonance should be balanced with factual accuracy. While stories engage the heart, data engages the mind. Including well-sourced statistics and verifiable information enhances your authority and ensures that your message holds up under scrutiny. Accuracy is key—any factual missteps may undermine the trust you've worked to build. When you successfully combine storytelling with solid facts, you deliver a well-rounded speech that appeals to both emotion and intellect.

As you prepare your next speech, consider how you can weave these elements together. Craft narratives that feature relatable characters, meaningful conflict, and clear resolution. Use emotional moments to connect, and draw from your own life or real-world examples to reinforce your message. Strike a thoughtful balance between storytelling and evidence.

When done well, this approach transforms a speech from a static presentation into a compelling, human conversation—one that your audience won't just listen to, but remember.

2.3 The Three-Act Model Structure

The three-act model structure is a powerful framework that can elevate your speech from a list of disjointed points into a cohesive, compelling story. Commonly used in literature, screenwriting, and storytelling, this structure is equally effective in public speaking, helping you deliver presentations, pitches, and speeches that captivate audiences. By breaking your content into three essential parts—setup, confrontation, and resolution—you create a clear narrative path that allows your audience to follow your message with ease.

In the first act, the setup, you lay the foundation for your speech. This is where you introduce your topic, providing context and preparing your listeners for the journey ahead. Here, you set the stage for what's to come, giving your audience an overview of the main points and establishing the significance of your message. A strong setup piques the audience's curiosity and gets them invested in the content of your speech.

The second act, confrontation, is where you delve into the heart of your message. This is the section where you present the core arguments, challenges, or conflicts that form the crux of your speech. It's the time to engage your audience with the depth of your ideas, providing evidence, examples, or stories that highlight the importance of the issue at hand. In this act, the audience should feel involved, questioning, and thinking critically about what you are saying.

Finally, the third act, resolution, ties everything together. This is where you bring closure to your speech, summarizing your key points and offering solutions, insights, or calls to action that leave a lasting impression. The resolution should not only wrap up the speech but also reinforce the message you want your audience to take away, ensuring it stays with them long after they've left.

When applying the three-act structure to your speech, consider your goals—whether to inform, persuade, or inspire. In an informative speech, the setup might involve defining key terms or providing background information. The confrontation would then present the main content, supported by evidence and examples, while the resolution would summarize the takeaways and reinforce your message.

In persuasive speeches, the setup might focus on establishing common ground with your audience, addressing a shared concern or issue. The confrontation would present your arguments and counter any opposing views, strengthening your case. The resolution would inspire your audience to take action or deeply reflect on the perspective you've shared, urging them to consider the next steps.

Smooth transitions between acts are vital for maintaining the flow of your speech. Using clear signposts can guide your audience through the structure, making it easy to follow your argument and stay engaged. Phrases like "Let's dive deeper into this" or "Now that we have the context, let's explore the challenges" help the audience track where you are in the speech and what's coming next. These signposts create a natural rhythm and keep listeners invested in your message.

A great example of the three-act structure in action is Steve Jobs' commencement speech at Stanford University on June 12, 2005. In the setup, Jobs introduced the theme of "connecting the dots," drawing his audience in with a personal story. The confrontation included stories of failure, loss, and eventual success, illustrating his unpredictable journey. The resolution tied all the elements together, delivering a powerful message about following your passion and finding purpose. Jobs' speech shows how the three-act structure can elevate a personal narrative into a universal lesson.

2.4 Create a Compelling Conclusion

The conclusion of a speech serves as the speaker's final opportunity to make a lasting impression on the audience. It is the point at which all preceding ideas converge into a coherent and powerful message—one that extends beyond the moment and continues to resonate with listeners. An effective conclusion does more than restate key arguments; it consolidates the central themes, reinforces the core message, and ensures the audience departs with a clear understanding of the speech's significance. Much like the final brushstroke that completes a painting, a well-crafted conclusion brings the entire presentation into focus.

Developing a memorable conclusion requires more than a summary. It should offer intellectual and emotional closure while also motivating the audience to engage with the content on a deeper level. A compelling conclusion often includes a call to action—an invitation for the audience to reflect, engage in dialogue, or enact change based on the ideas presented. By encouraging listeners to apply these insights to their own lives, the speaker fosters a sense of ownership and continuity. In doing so, the conclusion becomes a catalyst for action, transforming passive listeners into informed and empowered participants.

One highly effective rhetorical technique is to revisit themes or narratives introduced in the opening of the speech. This approach creates a sense of narrative symmetry, providing the audience with a satisfying sense of closure. By returning to the initial story, metaphor, or question, the speaker underscores the journey the audience has undertaken and reinforces the internal logic and coherence of the speech. This technique strengthens the thematic structure and enhances the emotional impact of the closing remarks.

Encouraging audience reflection is another powerful strategy. Posing open-ended, thought-provoking questions—such as "What steps will you take as a result of what you've heard today?"—promotes introspection and personal connection. Such prompts help the audience contextualise the speech within their own lives, thereby deepening its relevance and impact. Reflection anchors the message in lived experience and can be a decisive factor in whether the speech resonates in the long term.

Historical examples illustrate the power of a well-constructed conclusion. In his farewell address on 17 January 1961, President Dwight D. Eisenhower warned against the rise of the military-industrial complex, urging citizens to remain vigilant in preserving democratic values. His closing remarks distilled the essence of his message and issued a timeless call for civic responsibility. Similarly, following his release from prison, Nelson Mandela delivered speeches that emphasised reconciliation and national unity, concluding with hopeful visions that resonated far beyond the immediate audience. These speeches exemplify how a strategic conclusion can elevate a message from a momentary event to a lasting contribution to public discourse.

In sum, the conclusion of a speech should not be viewed as a mere formality but as a strategic opportunity to amplify its influence. Through purposeful summarisation, emotional resonance, narrative closure, and motivational appeal, a speaker can ensure that their message endures—both in memory and in action.

2.5 Master Your Body Language

Mastering body language is essential for becoming an effective speaker. It starts with your posture. Standing tall with shoulders back conveys confidence and authority, while your overall stance shows whether you are approachable or closed off. Facial expressions also play a crucial role; a genuine smile can make your audience more receptive to your message.

Using hand gestures effectively highlights your points and clarifies complex ideas. For example, instead of pointing your index finger directly at your audience, it's better to gesture upward. This approach feels more engaging and can help maintain a positive atmosphere.

They are not just extras but vital parts of your communication. Open body language, like uncrossed arms, signals openness, while crossed arms may imply defensiveness. Mirroring—subtly mimicking another person's gestures—can create a connection, building rapport and trust. However, it's important to be mindful of cultural differences; what signals openness in one culture might be interpreted differently in another.

Your body language must align with your words. If your gestures contradict your message, it can lead to mistrust. Your tone of voice should also complement your movements for a clear and believable delivery.

Gestures can powerfully enhance your communication by illustrating concepts that might be hard to explain. Imagine trying to describe something complex without using your hands; it would feel incomplete. The right gestures help emphasize key points and make your message more vivid, but be cautious—avoid repetitive movements that might distract your audience. Instead, synchronize your gestures with your speech to create a natural flow.

Maintaining eye contact and using facial expressions are fundamental for connecting with your audience. Eye contact shows confidence and engagement, but it's a balance—too little might seem evasive, while too much can feel intrusive. Distributing your gaze evenly across the room helps everyone feel included. Your facial expressions should match your words to maintain authenticity and avoid giving an impression of insincerity.

An interesting technique to boost your confidence is using power poses—expansive postures like standing with feet apart and hands on hips. Research suggests that adopting these poses can enhance feelings of power and reduce stress. Practicing power poses before a presentation can set a positive tone, so consider integrating them into your preparation by standing in front of a mirror and refining your presence.

In summary, mastering body language can significantly elevate your public speaking. It's about more than just what you say; it's how you convey your entire message. From posture to gestures, each element shapes how your audience perceives you. This chapter serves as a foundation for exploring vocal delivery in the next section.

Chapter 3:
Enhance Your Vocal Delivery

In Chapter 2, we explored how to build a well-structured speech—how organising your ideas with clarity and purpose can help your message land powerfully. But even the most brilliant structure needs the right voice to bring it to life. That's where vocal delivery comes in.

Think of your voice as the instrument that carries your message. The rise and fall of your tone, the pauses between your thoughts, the energy behind your words—these are the elements that turn a good speech into an unforgettable one. Without expressive delivery, even the most carefully crafted message can fall flat.

This chapter is all about helping you develop a voice that doesn't just speak but connects.

Just like athletes warm up before a race, warming up your voice is crucial for effectively delivering your message and protecting your vocal health. A well-prepared voice prevents strain and fatigue, enhances vocal range, and allows for clearer, more confident expression.

Vocal warm-ups are essential for keeping your voice in prime condition. Not only do they help reduce fatigue, but they also prevent hoarseness, especially during long presentations. Starting with lip trills and sirens gently engages your vocal cords, promoting flexibility and range. Lip trills relax the muscles around your mouth and throat, while humming acts as a gentle massage, improving both resonance and clarity. Humming also helps maintain a steady pitch and volume, ultimately enhancing the overall quality of your voice.

Tongue twisters are not just a fun activity—they're incredibly effective for improving diction and articulation. They challenge you to pronounce each sound clearly, helping you refine your speech and avoid mumbling. For instance, repeating phrases like "She sells seashells by the seashore" exercises your tongue, lips, and jaw, building clarity and boosting your confidence to speak fluently—even under pressure.

Incorporating physical exercises into your warm-up routine can also be highly beneficial. Simple neck and shoulder rolls release tension in your upper body, allowing your voice to flow more freely. A relaxed body significantly contributes to your vocal performance; when you feel at ease, your voice naturally follows suit, resulting in a more comfortable and confident delivery.

Lastly, customising your warm-up routine to fit your unique needs is key. Everyone's voice has specific tension points, so it's essential to identify where you typically feel tightness—whether it's your throat, jaw, or shoulders. Focus your exercises on these areas by adding targeted stretches or vocal drills. Personalising your routine ensures you can address challenges head-on, enabling you to deliver your message with clarity and confidence.

3.1 Vocal Warm-Up Checklist

1.   Lip Trills: Start gently to engage your vocal cords.

2.   Sirens: Watch your vocal range and enhance flexibility.

3.   Humming: Improve resonance and soften your vocal cords.

4.   Tongue Twisters: Sharpen your articulation and diction.

5.　　Neck and Shoulder Rolls: Release tension and promote relaxation.

6.　　Personal Customisation: Focus on your unique tension points for a tailored routine.

With this routine, you'll be ready to capture your audience with relative ease.

3.2 Master Your Voice Pitch and Tone

Consider a speaker whose voice holds your attention completely—rich with emotion, intent, and resonance—making each word seem vital and compelling. What creates this sense of captivation is not merely the content of the speech, but the speaker's vocal mastery, particularly their control over pitch and tone. These two vocal elements, when used effectively, can elevate speech delivery from a mechanical act to a memorable and emotionally engaging experience.

Pitch refers to the perceived frequency of sound—that is, how high or low a voice sounds—much like the musical notes on a scale. It introduces vocal variation, prevents monotony, and adds musicality to spoken language. Tone, on the other hand, conveys the speaker's emotional attitude or intent. It infuses words with nuance, helping the audience interpret not just what is being said, but how it is meant to be understood. If pitch is the melody of a speech, then tone is its mood. Understanding and controlling both elements is crucial for speakers seeking to maintain engagement and strengthen the impact of their message.

To cultivate effective pitch variation, one may borrow techniques from the world of music. Just as musicians warm up their instruments, speakers can prepare their voices by practising vocal scales—starting with a low hum and rising gradually to higher notes.

This practice not only warms the vocal cords but also enhances vocal agility and expressive range. Another beneficial exercise involves mimicking the melody of a familiar song during speech practice. This playful yet purposeful approach heightens one's awareness of natural pitch fluctuations and strengthens the ability to convey emotional shifts through vocal modulation.

Mastering tone is equally important and requires deliberate awareness of the emotional subtext carried by the voice. A warm, compassionate tone often evokes feelings of trust and empathy, allowing the speaker to establish a personal connection with the audience. It creates a sense of approachability and sincerity, qualities that are particularly valuable when discussing sensitive topics or offering support. When used authentically, such a tone enhances the speaker's credibility and fosters emotional resonance, encouraging listeners to engage more deeply with the message.

In contrast, a firm or assertive tone can be employed to emphasise urgency, underscore key messages, or convey authority. This tonal quality is especially effective when the speaker aims to prompt action, highlight the gravity of an issue, or guide the audience toward a particular course of thought. By intentionally alternating between warmth and assertiveness, a speaker can control the emotional tempo of the speech and shape the audience's interpretative experience.

Strategically varying both pitch and tone throughout a speech allows for multi-layered communication, in which information is delivered not only through words but through vocal expression. Statements that might otherwise seem simple or neutral gain rhetorical power, becoming memorable, persuasive, and emotionally charged. This vocal dynamism ensures that the speaker's ideas are not only heard but felt, forging a deeper connection between message and audience.

Ultimately, the skilful use of pitch and tone transforms spoken language into a full-bodied communicative act. It enables speakers to convey emotion, intention, and credibility simultaneously, making their delivery more impactful and enduring. In this way, the voice becomes not just a vehicle for speech, but a vital instrument of persuasion and human connection.

One of the most challenging experiences for both actors and preachers is the act of watching or listening to themselves perform. Many celebrities have openly discussed the discomfort and embarrassment they often feel when revisiting their interviews or performances. This reaction is quite common and perfectly natural. In my own experience, I've felt the same way.

Despite this unease, recording and critically listening to your speeches can lead to significant improvements in your public speaking abilities. By reviewing your recordings, you can gain valuable insights into how your audience perceives your pitch and tone. This exercise allows you to identify specific areas where you may come across as monotone, overly enthusiastic, or perhaps too harsh in your delivery.

Moreover, this process of self-evaluation can reveal patterns in your speaking style that may not be apparent at the moment. For instance, you might notice repetitive phrases or habits that could detract from your message. By pinpointing these aspects, you can make meaningful adjustments that enhance your overall effectiveness as a communicator. Engaging in this practice not only bolsters your confidence but also helps you develop a more authentic and engaging speaking persona over time.

To enhance your vocal expression, take the time to experiment with pitch and tone across various contexts. This intentional practice can significantly enrich the way you communicate. Consider engaging in mindful reading, a technique where you read aloud and consciously alter your pitch and tone to reflect a range of emotions—such as excitement, sadness, anger, or calmness. This not only helps in expanding your vocal range but also prepares you for a variety of speaking scenarios, whether in public speaking, presentations, or everyday conversations.

As you incorporate these techniques into your daily interactions, you strengthen their real-world application. It allows you to refine your skills in a natural setting, fostering a conversational style that maintains authenticity while also incorporating vocal variety. Make a habit of paying attention to your vocal delivery in different situations; notice how varying your pitch affects the mood and engagement levels of your listeners.

By diligently applying these strategies, you will cultivate a more dynamic and captivating speaking style. This not only enhances your ability to convey messages effectively but also strengthens your connection with the audience, making your communication more impactful and memorable. Over time, you'll find that your heightened awareness of vocal dynamics contributes to a greater confidence in your speaking abilities.

3.3 Articulate with Precision and Accuracy

Effective oral communication depends not only on what is said but also on how it is delivered. Among the most influential aspects of speech delivery are pitch, tone, articulation, and precision—each playing a distinct yet interconnected role in shaping how a message is received and understood. While pitch and tone infuse speech with emotional resonance and variety, articulation and precision ensure that the content is clearly conveyed and intelligible to a diverse audience. When listeners can easily follow along, they are more likely to trust the speaker's expertise and authority.

To improve your articulation, incorporating specific exercises into your practice routine is essential. For example, as a preacher of African descent living in the United Kingdom, I often receive feedback on my pronunciation during sermons. This constructive criticism has heightened my awareness of my diction and motivated me to refine my skills further as I prepare for each sermon.

In my presentations, I sometimes take a moment to demonstrate how one word can be pronounced in three different ways—African, British, and American. This not only enriches the understanding of my audience but also offers a valuable learning opportunity for anyone involved in public speaking. The significance of articulation and its role in communication will be explored further in Chapter 8, which is dedicated to cultural sensitivity and inclusivity in speech. By exploring these themes, we can better appreciate how language can be expressed and understood across diverse cultural contexts.

Another effective method for enhancing articulation is practicing consonant drills. Repeating tongue twisters like "Peter Piper picked a peck of pickled peppers" can help strengthen the muscles used in speech and improve clarity. Practicing vowel sounds is equally important. Focus on producing open, resonant vowels to prevent mumbling. Exercises such as elongating "AH" or "EE" help train your mouth and tongue to maintain clarity, even when speaking quickly.

Articulation challenges can arise from many sources. For instance, regional accents may enrich your speech but could be confusing to listeners unfamiliar with them. Practice striking a balance between your accent and clear communication, ensuring that your speech remains accessible to a wider audience. If you tend to speak quickly, try slowing down just a little—giving each word space will improve clarity.

Several tools and resources are available to help you practice and improve your articulation. Speech apps offer structured exercises with immediate feedback, making your practice more engaging and effective. Additionally, recording yourself can be highly beneficial. Listening to your recordings allows you to identify areas for improvement and track your progress over time.

Remember, articulation is a skill that anyone can develop with practice and dedication. By focusing on clear articulation, you ensure that your message is not only heard but understood. This clarity fosters a stronger connection with your audience, creating an environment where ideas flow freely and meaningfully, leaving a lasting impact on those who listen.

3.4 The Impact of Pauses for Effect

In a world filled with constant noise, the power of silence stands out. Pauses, when used strategically, can elevate your speech from a series of words to a memorable message. These pauses are not mere empty spaces; they are powerful tools that provide emphasis and clarity, allowing your key points to resonate deeply with your audience. When you pause, you create a sense of anticipation, inviting your listeners to lean in and focus on what comes next. Sometimes, this intentional silence communicates more effectively than words alone, offering your audience the opportunity to reflect and absorb your message fully.

Different types of pauses serve distinct purposes in enhancing your delivery. A dramatic pause can generate tension, leaving your audience on the edge of their seats, waiting for what's to come. Consider the impact of making a critical point, followed by a carefully timed silence—it allows the weight of your words to sink in. On the other hand, a reflective pause provides your audience with space to contemplate and engage with the message internally. After posing a thought-provoking question, stepping back gives them the room to process, deepening their engagement with your ideas.

Timing is crucial when incorporating pauses into your speech. A well-timed pause enhances the flow, while an ill-timed pause can disrupt it. Practicing with tools like a metronome can refine your sense of rhythm, helping you train your body to pause effectively. Observing natural conversations also provides valuable insights— people naturally pause to gather their thoughts or listen, and mirroring this rhythm in your delivery can make you feel more relatable and genuine.

However, it's important to use pauses wisely. Overusing them can make your speech feel disjointed, causing your audience to lose interest or giving the impression that you've forgotten what to say. The key is to balance pauses with fluidity, much like a well-composed piece of music, where the silence adds depth without interrupting the melody. Pauses should emphasize key points, but the flow of your speech should remain continuous and smooth.

To integrate pauses effectively, practice identifying key moments where a pause can amplify your message. This might occur before revealing an important idea or after telling a compelling story. As you practice, pay attention to how these pauses influence the rhythm and reception of your speech. Over time, you will develop an instinct for when and how long to pause, making your delivery more dynamic and engaging.

As you refine your use of pauses, always remember their essential role in shaping how your message is perceived and understood. Pauses allow you to transform your speech from a straightforward narrative into an engaging conversation that invites your audience to think and connect with your message. When used well, pauses can elevate your speech from ordinary to extraordinary.

Chapter 4:
Engage and Connect with Your Audiences

In Chapter 3, we focused on the importance of mastering your speech structure—organising your ideas in a way that flows logically and resonates with your audience. But what's the point of having a well-structured speech if you can't capture and hold your audience's attention? That's where the art of engagement comes into play.

Engagement goes beyond delivering your content—it's about creating a connection. Your audience is looking for more than just information; they want to feel something. They want to be drawn in, to relate to your message, and to feel invested in your story. Without engagement, even the best-structured speech can lose its impact.

In this chapter, you'll learn techniques for creating that connection, whether you're speaking to a room of ten or ten thousand. From understanding your audience's needs to using body language, eye contact, and stories that resonate, you'll discover how to keep your listeners engaged and make your message memorable.

In the realm of public speaking, establishing a genuine connection with your audience is of paramount importance. This connection transforms a mere delivery of information into an impactful experience that resonates emotionally with the listeners. To truly engage your audience, it is essential to recognise that effective communication goes beyond simply presenting facts or data; it involves creating a narrative that captivates and inspires.

Crafting a memorable experience starts with a deep understanding of your audience's needs, interests, and backgrounds. Take the time to research who will be in attendance—consider their demographics, expectations, and what they hope to gain from your speech. By tailoring your message to align with their values and interests, you can foster a sense of rapport and trust.

Again, instilling storytelling techniques, relatable examples, and interactive elements can further enhance engagement. Utilising eye contact, pauses, and vocal variety also plays a significant role in drawing your audience into the narrative. Ultimately, the goal is to leave them not just with information but with emotions and thoughts that linger long after your speech has concluded. The journey of effective public speaking begins with this foundational understanding of your audience and their unique perspectives.

Furthermore, knowing your audience is the key to effective communication. To connect with them, you must grasp the demographic landscape—age, interests, and cultural backgrounds all shape how your message will be received. For example, younger listeners may relate more to digital trends, while older audiences might appreciate historical context or practical applications. By recognising these differences, you can create a speech that respects and includes everyone.

Identifying your audience's needs and expectations is like preparing for a trip; you need a map to guide you. Pre-event surveys can be an excellent starting point, revealing what your audience hopes to learn and any questions they have. This insight allows you to tailor your presentation to address their primary concerns, making it more impactful. Additionally, reviewing feedback from past events can highlight what worked and what didn't, helping you refine your approach over time.

In our digital age, gathering audience insights is easier than ever. Tools like Sprout Social and BuzzSumo analyse social media data to reveal audience preferences and engagement patterns. Polling software can provide real-time feedback during your presentation, giving you an immediate understanding of your audience's thoughts. These resources help you connect more deeply with your listeners and tailor your message to their interests.

Once you've gathered this valuable information, the next step is to weave it into your speech. Customise your examples and stories based on what you've learned. If your research highlights a specific trend your audience cares about, include it. If there's a cultural theme that resonates, use it to frame your message. This attention to detail shows that you've considered your audience's world and helps forge a connection that goes beyond mere words.

4.1 Audience Research Checklist:

1.   Identify Demographics: Collect information on age, cultural background, and interests.

2.   Conduct Pre-Event Surveys: Ask your audience about their expectations and knowledge.

3.   Utilise Digital Tools: Use social media analytics and polling software for insights.

4.   Analyse Past Feedback: Look at previous audience responses to refine your approach.

5.   Customise Content: Tailor your speech with relevant examples and stories.

The art of engaging an audience lies in the details. It's about understanding who they are, what matters to them, and how they prefer to communicate. By investing time in this understanding, you lay the groundwork for a speech that informs, inspires, and connects deeply.

4.2 Create Audience-Centric Content

When you find yourself addressing a diverse audience, it's important to remember that each individual comes with their unique interests, backgrounds, and experiences. To truly engage this varied group, you need to take the time to connect your message with what resonates most deeply with them. By understanding the specific interests and concerns of your audience members, you can align your speech in a way that speaks to their values and priorities.

Rather than treating your presentation as a mere transmission of information, think of it as an opportunity for a meaningful dialogue. This approach allows you to transform an ordinary session into an interactive conversation, fostering a sense of connection and investment among your listeners. By sharing relevant anecdotes, incorporating relatable examples, and addressing topics that matter to them, you not only capture their attention but also encourage active participation and engagement throughout your presentation. Ultimately, tailoring your message to your audience elevates the experience, making it more impactful and memorable for everyone involved.

One effective way to engage your audience is by incorporating current industry trends. When you discuss the latest developments or breakthroughs, you show that you're in tune with what's happening right now. This not only grabs their attention but also creates a sense of relevance. Similarly, referencing recent events, whether they're technological advancements or societal changes, can make an immediate connection, allowing you to speak within a shared context with your audience.

Personalisation takes this connection further. By acknowledging specific audience members or their experiences, you create a warm atmosphere that feels engaging and inclusive. For example, mentioning a recent achievement of someone in the audience or relating your message to their experiences can invite them into your narrative, making it more relatable and impactful. Using names, relevant examples, and familiar scenarios can transform your speech into a personalised experience that resonates on a deeper level.

In addition to that, adjusting the complexity of your content is also crucial. Understanding your audience's knowledge level enables you to present information that is accessible yet informative. Avoiding technical jargon ensures that everyone feels included and prevents alienation. When dealing with complex topics, break them down into simpler parts and provide context or analogies. This enhances understanding and keeps the audience engaged, as they are more likely to stay interested when they can easily follow along.

More importantly, incorporating interactive elements further boosts engagement. Real-time polls and Q&A sessions can turn a one-way speech into a lively exchange. These activities invite your audience to participate, fostering a sense of involvement. Imagine asking a thought-provoking question and watching the room light up with discussion. This interactivity not only keeps the audience engaged but also gives you immediate feedback, allowing you to adjust your delivery as needed. Interactive case studies can also be effective, allowing the audience to explore real-life scenarios and apply the concepts you've discussed. These elements not only enhance the learning experience but also make your presentation memorable.

4.3 The Art of Storytelling

The power of storytelling is a remarkable force—an ancient art form that has stood the test of time and continues to captivate and inspire audiences across generations. Within the realm of public speaking, storytelling serves as a vital bridge that connects the speaker and the listener. By weaving narratives filled with relatable emotions and shared experiences, a speaker can create an atmosphere of intimacy and understanding. This connection not only captivates the audience's attention but also evokes empathy and engagement, allowing listeners to see the world through the speaker's perspective. The ability to transform facts and ideas into compelling stories can enhance the impact of the message being conveyed, making it more memorable and resonant. Through the art of storytelling, speakers are empowered to leave a lasting impression, forging deeper relationships with their audiences and igniting inspiration within them.

A well-crafted story fosters emotional connections, allowing listeners to step into the speaker's shoes and experience their journey. This connection creates empathy, transforming a simple speech into a meaningful exchange. But why do stories stick with us long after the details fade? It's because our brains remember narratives better than isolated facts. When you embed your message within a story, you give the audience a framework that makes the information easier to recall. Think of a story as a vessel carrying your core message on a journey that the audience can Visualise and relate to.

So, what makes a story compelling? At its core, a great tale features relatable characters facing challenges. These characters are essential; they bring the story to life and should resonate with the audience by embodying familiar traits or dilemmas. Whether they are overcoming obstacles or grappling with moral choices, their journeys reflect common human experiences. A clear and meaningful resolution provides closure and ties back to your central message, leaving the audience with a sense of understanding.

To create a lasting impact, use vivid imagery and sensory details. Describe the scent of rain on dry earth or the sound of leaves crunching beneath your feet, pulling the audience into your world. Pacing is also crucial—balance moments of excitement with pauses for reflection. Speeding up can build tension, while slowing down adds emotional depth, keeping your audience engaged throughout the story.

To infuse your storytelling with authenticity, consider incorporating personal anecdotes that vividly illustrate your experiences. This approach not only invites your audience to join you on your journey but also allows them to view the world through your perspective. By sharing your unique experiences, you create an intimate connection with your listeners, as they can relate to the emotions and lessons that shaped your narrative.

Moreover, the power of storytelling extends beyond personal experiences, resonating through universal themes that touch the human spirit. Concepts such as resilience—the ability to bounce back from adversity—and the deep, innate search for belonging resonate across diverse audiences. When you weave these themes into your narrative, you craft a tapestry of shared experiences that can inspire, uplift, and foster a sense of unity among your listeners, no matter their backgrounds.

Furthermore, storytelling in public speaking is far more than just an embellishment; it serves as a powerful vehicle for transformation and engagement. When you share stories, you establish a deep connection with your audience, reaching not only their intellect but also their emotions. This connection transforms abstract concepts into relatable experiences that resonate on a personal level.

As you weave storytelling into your speeches, it's essential to remember that your narrative has the potential to inspire change, educate listeners about important topics, and foster a sense of unity among diverse groups. Stories give life to ideas, making them tangible and memorable.

To create a truly captivating story, consider blending your insights with universal themes that many can relate to—love, struggle, triumph, or resilience. This combination enhances the relatability of your narrative and creates a shared experience that encourages your audience to reflect on their own lives.

Moreover, a well-crafted story can evoke emotions, solidifying your message in a way that statistics and facts alone cannot achieve. When your audience walks away, they won't just remember the details of your speech; they will carry with them the vivid imagery and emotions sparked by your storytelling long after you have finished speaking.

4.4 The Importance of Humour and Empathy

When you step onto a stage, humour becomes one of your greatest tools. It's more than just getting a laugh; it's about building a connection with your audience. Humour can turn a room full of strangers into a group of engaged listeners. A well-placed joke or a light-hearted comment can break the ice and ease the tension before you begin your speech.

Using humour can also make complex topics easier to understand. It adds a touch of relief, helping your audience digest difficult information without feeling overwhelmed. This doesn't mean making light of serious issues; rather, it allows you to present them in a relatable, human way.

Knowing when and how to use different types of humour is key to effective communication. For instance, self-deprecating humour makes you approachable and relatable, showing you don't take yourself too seriously but not in a negative way. It creates a bond with the audience, encouraging them to share in the laughter. On the other hand, observational humour highlights the quirky aspects of everyday life, making it a safe choice for diverse groups because it doesn't target anyone specifically.

However, it's crucial to use humour wisely. The goal is to engage, not to offend. Empathy plays a vital role in this process as well. By showing you understand and appreciate the emotions of your audience, you build trust and create a sense of community. Sharing relatable stories or acknowledging how your audience might feel can turn your presentation into a meaningful conversation rather than a one-sided lecture.

Striking the right balance between humour and sensitivity is especially important in diverse settings. Avoid jokes that could offend, as what's funny to one person may hurt another. Being aware of cultural differences and individual sensitivities is essential. Pay attention to your audience's reactions—body language, facial expressions, and verbal cues will guide you on whether to continue with your humour or pivot if a joke doesn't land.

Incorporating humour and empathy into your speeches does more than just lighten the mood—it profoundly enriches your message and forges a deeper bond with your audience. These elements transform what might be a simple presentation into a shared, memorable experience—one that's infused with laughter, understanding, and a sense of connection. Humour breaks down barriers, inviting your listeners to relax and open up, while empathy helps you resonate on a human level, fostering trust and emotional engagement. As you engage with your audience, remember that humour and empathy act as bridges, linking your message to their hearts and minds. They create a space where both speaker and listener are united in a common emotional and intellectual journey.

This chapter underscores the power of these tools in enhancing your public speaking, and in the next section, we'll dive into the art of time management—a crucial skill for ensuring your speech remains focused, engaging, and impactful.

Chapter 5:
Effective Time Management in Speeches

In the previous chapter, we delved into how to engage and connect with your audience, ensuring that your words resonate and hold their attention. But no matter how compelling your message is, time can be a tricky factor. How do you keep your audience engaged without overstaying your welcome? How do you deliver all your key points without rushing or dragging things out? The answer lies in effective time management.

Time management in a speech isn't just about sticking to the clock; it's about pacing your delivery, balancing content, and ensuring that every moment adds value to your message. A speech that drags on too long can cause your audience's attention to wane, while a rushed presentation can leave important points unspoken.

In this chapter, we'll explore strategies to help you make the most of the time you have. You'll learn how to prioritise your content, create natural transitions, and practice techniques for staying within your allotted time—without sacrificing impact. Because when you manage time well, you allow your message to land in the perfect way, with the perfect rhythm.

After all, it's not just what you say—it's how long you say it, and how effectively you say it in the time you have.

Just as a traveller meticulously plans and coordinates various elements to ensure they catch their flight at the busy airport—

checking in on time, navigating security lines, and arriving at the correct gate—public speaking requires a similar level of precision and forethought. In this scenario, time serves as your runway, providing the necessary space to prepare and deliver your message effectively. Managing your time wisely is essential, as it helps you structure your speech, engage your audience, and convey your key points with clarity and impact. Mastering the art of timing not only enhances the strength of your presentation but also helps to establish a connection with your listeners, ensuring that your message is both memorable and persuasive.

The first step in effective time management is gaining a clear understanding of your time constraints. Knowing exactly how long you have allowed you to craft your speech with precision, ensuring it fits seamlessly into the allotted time. Start by reviewing the event schedule—not only for your speaking slot but also to understand how it aligns with the broader program. This awareness helps you anticipate potential delays and adjust accordingly. Equally important is maintaining clear communication with the event organisers. Confirm your time limit and inquire about any flexibility. Taking a proactive approach not only helps you avoid surprises but also sets the foundation for a smooth, well-paced presentation that respects both your audience and the event's flow.

Creating a detailed speech outline is essential for managing your time. An outline serves as a roadmap, helping you balance your introduction, body, and conclusion. Allocate time for each section to maintain this balance and resist the urge to spend too long on any one point. Practicing with a timer can help you gauge your pacing, revealing areas to speed up or slow down. This practice not only keeps you on track but also boosts your confidence, allowing you to engage your audience more effectively.

Blending buffer time into your speech is another strategic and often overlooked tactic. Just as a seasoned traveller accounts for potential delays, a skilled speaker builds in space for unexpected moments. This buffer time serves multiple purposes: it can accommodate technical issues, provide room for audience interaction, or allow for impromptu thoughts and adjustments. By allowing for these pauses, your presentation feels less like a monologue and more like a dynamic dialogue. These moments show respect for your audience's input, fostering a deeper connection and enhancing the impact of your message.

Moreover, these pauses do more than just fill time—they enable you to adapt to the mood of the room, making your speech feel more fluid and natural. Whether it's letting laughter settle after a humorous anecdote or pausing for a moment of reflection after an important point, buffer time makes your delivery more conversational and engaging.

Prioritising your key points is equally critical. Not every detail in your speech carries the same weight or importance. To maintain focus and clarity, it's essential to identify and prioritise the core ideas you want your audience to remember. This doesn't mean eliminating supporting information entirely, but rather recognising which elements are truly vital and which ones can be trimmed if time is tight. A well-structured speech makes it easy to pinpoint where you can cut, ensuring that even if you need to adjust on the fly, your audience still walks away with a clear understanding of your central message.

This process of prioritisation streamlines your delivery and allows you to craft a focused, powerful narrative. By honing in on what matters most, you ensure that your message not only resonates with your audience but sticks with them long after you've finished speaking.

5.1 Practice your Speech with Precision

Rehearsing your speech is indispensable for managing time effectively. The more familiar you are with the rhythm and flow of your presentation, the more naturally you can adjust during the actual speech. Practicing ensures that each part of your speech gets the right emphasis and that you are mindful of pacing from beginning to end. Conducting full practice runs allows you to experience the entire speech in real time, giving you a sense of how it unfolds. This gives you the opportunity to identify sections that may feel too rushed or overly drawn out, offering you a chance to make adjustments that keep the flow intact.

Recording your rehearsals is an invaluable tool in your preparation. Listening or watching yourself from an audience's perspective provides critical feedback on your timing, delivery, and content. You'll be able to pinpoint exactly where you need to speed up or slow down, where pauses are too long or too short, and whether you're hitting your key points effectively. This external perspective is crucial in refining your presentation and ensuring that your delivery is not only well-paced but also engaging. With this insight, you can stay within your time constraints without sacrificing the quality of your message, making sure your audience remains captivated from start to finish.

Using tools like stopwatches or timer apps can greatly assist you in managing your speech timing. These digital tools help you keep track of how long you spend on each part, with timer apps on smartphones providing convenience and flexibility. Visual reminders, such as colour-coded cards or on-screen timers, can also help you stay on pace without disrupting your flow. This way, you can focus on delivering your message rather than constantly checking the clock.

Simulating real conditions during practice can further enhance your timing. Practicing in front of a mirror allows you not only to rehearse your speech but also to observe your body language and ensure it complements your message. Better yet, practicing in front of friends or family can provide valuable real-time feedback on your timing and how it affects audience engagement. Additionally, try to replicate the acoustics of your venue while practicing. This will help you adjust your volume and pacing accordingly, reducing any surprises during the actual event.

As you refine your speech, be ready to make adjustments based on the feedback you receive. You may find certain sections are too long or too short, which calls for editing. Cutting out repetitive content is an effective way to streamline your presentation; redundancy wastes time and can dilute your message. Conversely, achieving a balance between clarity and brevity is crucial. Strive to make your points concise but still rich in content. Simplifying complex ideas or using straightforward language can help ensure your audience grasps the main points without feeling overwhelmed.

5.2 Interactive Element: Timing Practice Checklist

1.   Full-Length Rehearsals: Practice your speech from beginning to end, focusing on parts that need better pacing.

2.   Record and Review: Record your rehearsals to identify timing issues and areas that can be improved.

3.   Timing Tools: Use a stopwatch or timer app to keep track of your speech duration accurately.

4.   Visual Cues: Add subtle reminders to help you monitor time without being distracting.

5.   Real-World Simulation: Rehearse in front of a mirror or a small audience to replicate real conditions.

6.   Acoustic Awareness: Choose a practice space that mimics the acoustics of your actual venue.

7.   Content Refinement: Edit your speech to remove any repetitive sections and enhance clarity.

By using these strategies, you'll manage your time effectively and deliver a speech that connects with your audience.

5.3 Adapt On-the-Fly

Imagine standing just moments away from delivering a carefully crafted speech—only to be informed that your time slot has changed, your audience has shifted, or a key part of the programme has been unexpectedly altered. How would you respond? In the unpredictable world of public speaking, such last-minute adjustments are far from rare. They demand not only composure but also the crucial ability to adapt swiftly and effectively.

One of the most valuable skills a speaker can cultivate is the capacity to modify their presentation in real time while still maintaining clarity, coherence, and audience engagement. This begins with reading the room. As you speak, observe your audience closely. Non-verbal cues—such as furrowed brows, fidgeting, or distant gazes—can reveal whether your message is resonating or missing the mark. If you detect confusion, it may be necessary to pause and clarify a point. If disengagement sets in, consider shifting your delivery: vary your tone, tell a story, or introduce an interactive moment to regain attention.

Being responsive to these cues allows you to adjust the rhythm and structure of your speech with finesse. Perhaps you need to slow down and elaborate on a concept, or conversely, accelerate to maintain momentum. Either way, attuning yourself to the audience's feedback enables you to turn what might otherwise be an awkward or disjointed moment into a compelling opportunity for connection.

Unexpected changes to timing are another frequent occurrence. You may suddenly be granted more time than anticipated—providing a chance to enrich your talk with additional stories, real-life examples, or audience interaction. On the other hand, if your allotted time is reduced at short notice, you must be able to distil your message on the spot. This requires discernment: which elements are essential to your core message, and which can be summarised or omitted without compromising the integrity of your talk?

Ultimately, adaptability is not about improvising aimlessly, but about remaining anchored to your purpose while adjusting your delivery to meet the moment. By learning to think and speak on your feet, you enhance your authority, build trust, and ensure that your audience walks away with the message you intended to convey—no matter the circumstances.

Staying calm under pressure is particularly crucial in these moments of potential disruption. It's natural to feel a surge of anxiety when faced with the unexpected, but cultivating a sense of inner peace can help you remain focused and composed. Techniques such as mindful breathing—taking slow, intentional breaths to centre yourself—can significantly lower your heart rate and clear any mental fog, allowing you to think clearly and respond thoughtfully to the situation at hand. Confidence in your material is equally important; profound familiarity with your content empowers you to present it smoothly and with conviction, even in challenging circumstances.

Many distinguished speakers—such as those gracing the TED stage—boldly demonstrate how to manage unforeseen hurdles, including technical difficulties or abrupt schedule changes. One of their hallmark traits is their ability to pivot gracefully, showcasing their thorough preparation. For example, if a microphone fails, a skilled speaker might deliver a powerful anecdote that doesn't depend on technology, or if the time suddenly shifts, they could reorganise their presentation on the spot. This adaptability not only keeps the audience engaged but also exemplifies the speaker's preparedness and poise.

The ability to adjust in real-time is a crucial skill for any speaker, transforming potential setbacks into opportunities for deeper connection with the audience. When you're able to navigate unexpected changes with confidence, it not only maintains the flow of your presentation but also reinforces your message's relevance and impact. By adapting on the fly, you demonstrate your flexibility and expertise, ensuring that the core of your message resonates clearly, no matter what challenges arise.

As you become more seasoned in recognising and responding to these variables, your delivery will grow stronger and more effective. Each adjustment you make enhances your ability to engage with your audience, creating a dynamic and memorable experience. Over time, this adaptability not only strengthens your connection with listeners but also elevates your public speaking skills, leaving a lasting impression that lingers long after the speech is over.

5.4 Balance Brevity and Depth

See yourself at a banquet where the table is brimming with delicious dishes. You're excited to try everything but realise you can't possibly eat it all. This is similar to the challenge of balancing content in your speech. You have a wealth of information and stories to share, but time is limited.

The key is to find the right balance between being thorough and being concise. Overloading your audience with information can lead to confusion and fatigue, causing them to lose interest. Clarity is essential; you want your main message to shine through clearly, allowing the audience to grasp your core ideas.

One effective way to communicate concisely is to use bullet points and lists. These tools break down complex ideas into digestible bites, helping your audience follow along easily. Plus, using analogies can make difficult concepts more relatable. For example, comparing a complicated financial model to a household budget helps make the topic more approachable. These techniques not only streamline your delivery but also enhance retention by making your message more memorable.

While being concise is important, there are moments when diving deeply into a key topic is necessary. The trick is to explore these areas without running out of time. Focus on impactful examples that illustrate your points vividly rather than overwhelming your audience with statistics and details. Strive for clarity and depth, emphasizing critical insights to ensure your audience grasps your main message.

Feedback is an essential tool for refining the balance of your content. After your speech, actively seek input to gauge whether your message was clear, engaging, or if certain parts felt overwhelming. This feedback serves as a roadmap for improving your future presentations, helping you pinpoint areas that may need adjustment. In addition to content feedback, analysing your timing can reveal whether you lingered too long on specific sections, potentially causing your audience to lose focus or interest.

Keep in mind that every audience and topic is unique. What resonates with one group may not be as effective with another, so it's crucial to remain flexible in your approach. The art of balancing brevity with depth lies in understanding your audience's needs and adjusting your content accordingly. This ensures that your message is not only delivered but is impactful, leaving a lasting impression on your listeners.

As we move forward to the next chapter, we will dive into strategies for building confidence in your content. This will empower you to deliver speeches that are not only engaging and clear but also captivating and inspiring.

Chapter 6:
How To Build Confidence In Content

In the previous chapter, we explored the importance of effective time management in delivering a speech. With the right pacing, you can ensure your message lands with precision and impact. But even the most perfectly timed speech can fall short if you don't have the confidence in your content. After all, a confident speaker exudes authority, and when you're confident in your message, your audience is more likely to believe in it too.

Building confidence in your content starts with truly understanding it. The more deeply you know your material, the more assured you'll feel when presenting it. Confidence isn't about memorizing every word; it's about knowing your message so well that it becomes second nature. When you're secure in your content, you're free to focus on delivery and connection, instead of worrying about what comes next.

In this chapter, we'll uncover techniques for building that confidence—through preparation, practice, and understanding the value of your message. You'll learn how to connect with your material in a way that transforms uncertainty into conviction. Because when you're confident in your content, you won't just inform your audience—you'll inspire them.

Delivering a compelling speech is no different from diving into the unknown. It requires courage, conviction, and most importantly, confidence—not only in your delivery but in the content you're about to present. That confidence doesn't come out of nowhere; it's built slowly and intentionally, brick by brick, with one key ingredient: solid, trustworthy research.

Before you step onto any stage, your message must be anchored in understanding. Research is the bedrock of any impactful speech. It's what transforms vague ideas into powerful narratives. It lends weight to your words and shapes your credibility—the invisible force that makes an audience lean in, listen, and believe.

Think of credibility as the scaffolding of your authority. It evolves throughout your speech and is made up of three core components:

•   Initial credibility is what you bring to the table before you even speak—your qualifications, reputation, and perceived trustworthiness.

•   Derived credibility is built as you speak, through the strength of your arguments, the richness of your examples, and the quality of your sources.

•   Terminal credibility is the impression you leave behind—what lingers in your audience's minds after the applause fades.

The more thoroughly you research, the stronger each form of credibility becomes. Drawing from diverse, credible sources is like layering your speech with armour. Academic journals offer depth and rigor; interviews with experts inject personal and professional insight; government publications and NGO reports provide vetted statistics that root your claims in reality. A well-researched speech doesn't just inform—it persuades, convinces, and connects.

Research is also your secret weapon for anticipating tough questions and countering scepticism. When your audience sees that you've considered different perspectives and accounted for nuances, their trust in you deepens. You're no longer just a speaker—you become a guide through complex terrain.

But gathering information is only half the journey. Organising that research is what transforms chaos into clarity. Imagine setting out on a road trip with no GPS, no map, not even a list of stops. That's what a speech without structure feels like. Disorganised data can overwhelm you and confuse your audience. Creating tools like annotated bibliographies helps keep your sources at your fingertips. Digital tools like Zotero or EndNote allow you to manage citations, attach PDFs, and jot down quick thoughts—all in one place, streamlining your workflow and ensuring that no gem of information gets lost.

Just as important as collecting and organising data is avoiding the common traps of weak research. Not all sources are created equal. Understanding the difference between primary and secondary sources can safeguard the integrity of your message. Primary sources—first-hand accounts, original studies, and direct interviews—offer raw, unfiltered evidence. Secondary sources analyse and interpret that data, adding context. Always double-check authenticity and cross-reference facts. A single unreliable source can compromise your entire message, like a weak rung on a ladder.

In the end, a well-prepared speaker doesn't just speak—they deliver. They inform with authority, persuade with power, and connect with authenticity. Your audience will feel that they're in good hands because you've done the work. You've climbed the ladder, taken a breath, and launched off the edge with purpose and preparation.

And when you land—smoothly, confidently—the splash you make will ripple far beyond the surface.

Resource List: Tools for Organising Research

• Annotated Bibliographies: Create detailed entries summarizing the relevance of each source.

• Zotero: A user-friendly tool to organise and cite your sources easily.

• Primary vs. Secondary Sources: Accurately categorize and reference your sources.

By weaving these elements together, you build a strong framework that enhances your ability to communicate effectively and with conviction.

Making Your Case Persuasively

Persuasion in public speaking isn't just about *what* you say—it's about *how* you say it. A persuasive speech, when crafted and delivered with intention, becomes more than just a presentation of facts. It turns into an experience that captures attention, stirs emotion, and inspires action.

At the core of every persuasive speech are three timeless elements: ethos, pathos, and logos. These work together to create a balanced, compelling message that connects with your audience on multiple levels.

Ethos is your credibility—the sense of trust and integrity your audience feels when they believe you're both knowledgeable and sincere. It isn't just your credentials or expertise, but the way you show up: your tone, your transparency, your relatability. Sharing personal stories is a powerful way to build ethos. When you open up about a real experience—a struggle, a turning point, a lesson learned—you invite the audience into your world. You're no longer just a speaker; you become someone they can see themselves in. That connection lays the groundwork for trust.

Pathos, on the other hand, reaches the heart. It's about emotion—the ability to make your audience feel something that stays with them long after the speech is over. Whether it's through a vivid story, a vulnerable moment, or a well-timed pause, pathos invites empathy. It allows your message to resonate deeply. People may forget your facts, but they rarely forget how you made them feel. And in that emotional connection, transformation can begin.

Then comes logos—the logic, the structure, the proof. Logos provides the backbone of your argument, grounding your message in facts, statistics, and reasoned analysis. It's where you walk your audience through the "why" and "how" of your point, using clear examples and strong reasoning. This can involve deductive logic—starting with a general truth and narrowing it down to a specific conclusion—or inductive logic—gathering specific observations to build a broader insight. When done well, your audience follows your thought process step by step, feeling guided and informed rather than overwhelmed.

A key part of persuasive speaking also involves recognizing and addressing counterarguments. Instead of ignoring opposing views, acknowledge them. This shows that you're not just pushing a viewpoint—you're engaged in a thoughtful, balanced discussion. When you anticipate objections and respond with calm, well-supported responses—using data, expert insight, or personal testimony—you not only strengthen your position, you enhance your credibility.

And then, like seasoning in a rich dish, rhetorical devices elevate your message. These tools add rhythm, imagery, and impact. Metaphors and analogies help simplify complex ideas, turning abstract points into relatable, visual experiences. Comparing your argument to a journey, a puzzle, or a planted seed helps your audience understand and remember your message more clearly. Repetition is another powerful technique. When you echo key phrases or themes, you reinforce your message and make it stick. A line repeated with intention can become a heartbeat in your speech—something your audience holds onto.

When all of these elements come together—credibility, emotion, logic, thoughtful counterpoints, and artistic delivery—you create more than a speech. You create a moment. A persuasive speech isn't just heard; it's felt, remembered, and acted upon.

Proving the Value of Your Content

To ensure your message truly resonates with your audience, it's essential to start with a deep understanding of who they are, what they value, and what they hope to gain from your presentation. One of the most effective ways to achieve this is by conducting pre-speech surveys. These surveys can provide valuable insights into your audience's interests, pain points, expectations, and even preferred communication styles. The data you gather helps you shape your content in a way that speaks directly to their needs, increasing the likelihood of meaningful engagement and long-term impact.

But preparation doesn't stop there. Analysing feedback from your past presentations—whether through formal evaluations, follow-up conversations, or audience engagement metrics—offers another layer of insight. Patterns in feedback can illuminate what resonated most, what may have caused confusion, and what fell flat. This allows you to continuously evolve as a speaker, building on your strengths while addressing areas for improvement.

Once you've gathered and synthesized this information, it's incredibly beneficial to share your draft speech with a circle of trusted peers or mentors. Their external perspective can provide constructive criticism, offer fresh ideas, and challenge you to push your content further. This peer review stage acts as a rehearsal, allowing you to refine your messaging, tone, structure, and delivery before stepping in front of your audience.

This approach is not just about preparation—it's about transformation. By investing in audience research, reflection, and feedback, you're not merely crafting a better talk; you're becoming a more thoughtful, responsive, and impactful communicator. We'll delve deeper into this concept of transformative practice and the art of leveraging feedback in Chapter 10, where we explore how intentional iteration can elevate your speaking skills to the next level.

Keeping your content relevant also means staying updated on current events and trends. By linking your message to recent developments, you demonstrate awareness of the broader context, making your speech more compelling. For example, discussing recent advancements in technology can enhance your credibility and position you as an informed speaker.

Incorporating these strategies enables you to craft a speech that not only informs but also captivates, ensuring your message lands with clarity, purpose, and resonance. One of the most powerful tools at your disposal is timeliness—delivering content that feels relevant to the moment. Whether it's a trending issue, a timely anecdote, or a reference to recent events, relevance grabs attention and encourages your audience to lean in from the very beginning.

Equally important is the ability to adapt your content to different contexts. In professional or academic settings, a formal tone, structured delivery, and the use of industry-specific data lend credibility and authority to your message. In more casual environments, however, a conversational tone that includes humour, personal narratives, or even moments of vulnerability can create a deeper emotional connection with your audience. Flexibility in your communication style isn't just a bonus—it's a necessity for effective public speaking.

Cultural sensitivity is another crucial element of impactful communication. Every culture carries its own set of norms, values, and expectations, and being attuned to these differences helps you avoid missteps and fosters mutual respect. A message that is mindful of cultural dynamics not only avoids alienation but builds trust, allowing you to connect with a broader, more diverse audience.

Moreover, validating your message is not a one-time task; it is an ongoing, dynamic process. Relevance is not static—it shifts with context, audience needs, and time. This is why continuous reflection and refinement are key. Regularly assessing your content, seeking feedback from diverse sources, and being willing to revise your approach ensures your message remains impactful, adaptable, and meaningful, no matter the audience.

Ultimately, these strategies contribute to a cycle of growth: you listen, learn, and evolve. By embracing adaptability, cultural awareness, and a mind-set of continuous improvement, you position yourself not just as a speaker, but as a communicator who resonates—consistently and authentically.

Tailor Your Content for Impact

To connect with your audience in a way that's both meaningful and memorable, think of your message as a custom-tailored suit—it should fit the unique shape of their interests, challenges, and expectations with precision and care. Generic content can only go so far. Audiences are more perceptive than ever, and they can tell when a message is designed for someone else. This makes it essential to step into their shoes and ask: *What are they hoping to gain?* Are they looking for practical solutions to pressing problems? Do they need clarity around shifting industry trends, or are they seeking inspiration, motivation, and personal growth? By honing in on these specific desires and concerns, you transform your presentation from a generic delivery into a rich, targeted experience—one that feels personally designed for each listener.

But great communication isn't just about offering answers—it's about showing that you understand the questions. Recognising shared challenges is a powerful way to build rapport and establish trust early in your speech. Whether your audience is grappling with burnout, navigating change, balancing priorities, or facing uncertainty about the future, naming those pain points helps you bridge the emotional distance. You demonstrate empathy, which is foundational to connection. Suddenly, your audience sees you not as an outsider, but as someone who's walked in their shoes. This shift transforms your talk from a monologue into a dynamic conversation—one that says, *"I get you, and I'm here to offer something that matters."*

At the heart of this emotional resonance lies one of the oldest and most powerful communication tools ever known: storytelling. Stories don't just convey information—they create connection. They help audiences *feel* what you're saying, not just understand it. Stories allow your ideas to breathe, take shape, and become real in the minds of listeners. To harness the full power of storytelling, focus on crafting narratives that echo your audience's realities.

Create characters who reflect their values, struggles, and aspirations. Whether the story is personal, borrowed, or hypothetical, it should highlight real emotions, decisions, and transformations. Describe the setting with vivid sensory detail—the texture of the moment, the emotion in the air. Use metaphors and anecdotes that anchor your message in lived experience. A well-told story becomes the bridge that carries your message directly into your audience's memory and heart.

To further enhance the connection, integrate visual aids that complement your message. Humans are visual creatures—our brains process images significantly faster than text. When used purposefully, visual elements like slides, graphics, videos, and even props can clarify, emphasize, and bring your ideas to life. But remember: less is often more. Clean, uncluttered slides with strong imagery and minimal text allow your audience to stay focused on your words. Avoid overwhelming them with data dumps or complicated charts—instead, break down information into visually digestible formats. Infographics, timelines, and comparison visuals are especially effective for simplifying complex concepts and reinforcing key takeaways. When visuals and storytelling work together, they engage both the logical and emotional sides of your audience's brain, leading to deeper understanding and stronger retention.

Yet, even the most compelling speech is only as effective as its impact—and this can only be known through reflection. After your presentation, take time to measure your effectiveness. Pay close attention to how your audience responded in real time: Did they nod in agreement, take notes, laugh at your humour, or ask thoughtful questions? These subtle cues reveal engagement levels. More formally, ask for feedback—both structured (via surveys or forms) and informal (through conversation). Look for patterns in what people found most meaningful or confusing. And perhaps most importantly, engage in self-reflection. How did you feel delivering the speech? When did you feel in flow? Were there any moments that fell flat or didn't connect the way you hoped? Your own perceptions, paired with external feedback, provide a full picture of how your message landed—and what you can do better next time.

Ultimately, tailoring your presentation for maximum impact is about far more than preparation—it's a commitment to intentional, human-centred communication. It means seeing your audience not as passive receivers of content, but as active participants in an experience you're creating. When you take the time to understand their needs, connect through authentic storytelling, use visuals wisely, and reflect deeply, you don't just deliver a presentation— you create a lasting impression.

Every audience is different. Every setting is unique. But when you lead with empathy, insight, and clarity, you position yourself not just as a speaker—but as a guide, a connector, and a catalyst for meaningful change.

Chapter 7:
Leverage Technology for Smooth Presentations

In the previous chapter, we focused on building confidence in your content, ensuring that you're not only knowledgeable but also secure in what you're presenting. But in today's digital age, confidence in your material isn't enough—you also need to harness the power of technology to elevate your presentation. After all, the right tools can amplify your message, engage your audience, and help you manage the unexpected.

Whether it's using multimedia to enhance your points, integrating interactive elements, or ensuring smooth transitions between slides, technology can transform a good presentation into a great one. But like any powerful tool, it requires skilful handling. You need to know how to use it effectively to support—not distract from—your message.

In this chapter, we'll explore how to leverage various technologies, from presentation software like PowerPoint and Prezi to interactive tools and apps that boost engagement. You'll learn how to seamlessly integrate these elements into your presentation, so you can focus on delivering your message while technology works for you, not against you.

The beauty of technology in public speaking is much like stepping onto a stage where your words come to life—not just through your voice, but through a rich tapestry of visuals, sounds, and movement. Imagine your presentation transforming into a vibrant experience, filled with dynamic images, compelling videos, and interactive elements that pull your audience into your message. This is the magic that unfolds when you master modern presentation tools—your speech becomes more than a talk; it becomes an immersive journey.

In today's digital age, the tools at our fingertips can elevate even the simplest message into something truly unforgettable. Whether you're a seasoned presenter or just starting out, your ability to leverage technology can dramatically influence how your message is received and remembered. It's no longer just about what you say—it's about how you present it. A well-designed slide deck or a thoughtful integration of multimedia can capture attention, boost understanding, and increase emotional engagement.

Among the many tools available, several stand out for their unique capabilities and ease of use:

Microsoft PowerPoint remains a trusted staple. Known for its depth and versatility, it allows for detailed customisation—from animations and transitions to embedded videos and charts. Its broad feature set can help you build a professional, well-structured presentation, though the sheer number of options can sometimes be overwhelming for beginners.

Prezi offers a more cinematic storytelling experience. Unlike traditional slide-by-slide formats, Prezi uses a zoomable canvas that lets you pan across topics in a visually fluid way. This creates a sense of movement and narrative flow, making it especially effective for thematic or concept-driven presentations.

Canva is ideal for those who value design and simplicity. With its drag-and-drop interface, rich template library, and access to thousands of graphics, it empowers users—even those without a design background—to create visually stunning presentations quickly and easily.

Each of these platforms has its own strengths, and your choice should reflect your personal style, your message, and the expectations of your audience. The key is to select a tool that complements—not complicates—your delivery.

But remember, technology is only as powerful as your ability to use it well. Creating an effective presentation goes far beyond selecting a platform. It's about crafting a cohesive and intentional visual experience that enhances your message, not distracts from it.

Start by choosing a theme or template that aligns with your tone and purpose. A consistent visual identity—fonts, colours, and imagery—creates a polished look that reinforces your credibility. Customise these elements to reflect your brand or personality. Thoughtful use of white space, proper text alignment, and colour contrast will improve readability and keep your slides clean and engaging.

Your visuals should always *support* your content. Charts should simplify complex ideas. Photos should evoke emotion or context. Videos should reinforce your points, not serve as filler. Avoid cluttered slides or blocks of text that compete with your spoken words. Instead, aim for a minimalist design that gives your message room to breathe while enhancing clarity.

To create true impact, integrate your visual elements strategically throughout your speech. Think of them as rhythm and punctuation—adding energy, focus, and pause when needed. When done right, your visuals will guide your audience's attention, highlight key ideas, and deepen their emotional and intellectual connection to your message.

In the end, mastering presentation technology is about more than just technical skill—it's about **intention and creativity**. When used thoughtfully, these tools help you communicate with clarity, authenticity, and style. They allow you to bring your message to life in a way that is engaging, memorable, and uniquely yours.

So, embrace the technology at your fingertips—not as a crutch, but as a creative partner in your storytelling. When you combine a well-crafted message with compelling visuals, you transform your presentation into a powerful experience your audience won't soon forget.

For increasing interactivity, consider adding multimedia elements such as videos and audio clips to keep your audience engaged and cater to different learning styles. Interactive polls can turn your presentation into a dialogue, inviting feedback and participation, making it a dynamic exchange rather than a one-sided lecture.

Efficiency in creating your presentation is also key, especially when time is tight. Learn keyboard shortcuts for quicker navigation and use drag-and-drop features for easy customisation. These tips help you save time and focus more on refining your content rather than overcoming technical obstacles. With the right tools and techniques, you can elevate your presentations to captivate any audience.

7.1 Interactive Element: Software Mastery Checklist

Explore Tools: Experiment with Microsoft PowerPoint, Google Slides, or Keynote to find the platform that aligns best with your style and needs.

Customise Templates: Adjust fonts, colours, and design elements to reflect your brand or personal taste, ensuring your presentation feels authentic.

Integrate Multimedia: Enhance your message by adding videos, audio clips, and other multimedia elements to reinforce key points.

Engage with Polls: Incorporate interactive polls or questions to boost audience participation and make your presentation more dynamic.

Utilise Shortcuts: Familiarize yourself with keyboard shortcuts to speed up navigation and editing, improving efficiency during creation and delivery.

By utilising these techniques, you can elevate your presentations, transforming them into engaging experiences that leave a memorable impact on your audience.

7.2 Handle Technical Glitches without fear

What do you do when you're about to present in a packed room, and suddenly, the screen goes blank? This common nightmare can strike fear into even the most prepared presenters. Technical glitches, such as a projector failing or an audio malfunction, can derail your carefully crafted message in an instant. The key to navigating these challenges is knowing what to expect and being ready to act when things go wrong.

Projector and display issues often top the list—whether it's syncing your device, dealing with an unfocused display, or the dreaded blank screen. Audio problems, such as a microphone cutting out or unwanted feedback, can be just as disruptive. By anticipating these potential issues, you can minimize the risk of losing your audience's attention when technology fails.

Creating a backup plan is not just a smart move—it's essential. If your slides refuse to load or your laptop decides to update unexpectedly, you need a contingency strategy. Printed handouts can be a lifesaver, ensuring you can still communicate key points if the screen goes dark. Carrying a portable projector is another great precaution. Compact and easy to transport, it can serve as a backup if the venue's equipment malfunctions. Think of it as a spare tire for your car: something you hope you'll never need, but you'll be thankful for it if the unexpected happens.

Incorporating these safeguards into your preparation allows you to present confidently, knowing you're ready for anything, and ensuring your message gets through even when the technology doesn't cooperate.

When technical difficulties arise, quick thinking becomes your best friend. Start by checking your cable connections—a loose HDMI or power cable can cause many problems. Sometimes, simply restarting your devices can solve minor glitches, much like hitting the reset button on a stubborn gadget.

Preparation goes beyond backup plans; it also means getting familiar with the equipment. Practicing with your presentation tools is crucial. Conduct dry runs to ensure you can operate everything smoothly, from setting up the projector to adjusting microphone levels. Checking device compatibility is equally important; make sure your computer works well with the venue's systems. This proactive approach helps minimize surprises on the big day, allowing you to concentrate on delivering your message.

Technology can be both helpful and challenging in presentations. While it enhances communication, it can also introduce complications that interrupt your flow. By understanding these challenges and preparing for them, you can stay calm and keep your audience engaged, no matter what hiccups occur.

The Importance of Engaging with Virtual Audiences

In today's digital age, connecting with your audience through virtual platforms is not just a convenience—it's an essential part of effective communication. Whether you're hosting a webinar, conducting a training session, or delivering a keynote speech, leveraging the right virtual tools can significantly elevate the engagement and impact of your presentation. Understanding the features of popular virtual presentation platforms is key to ensuring your message is both compelling and interactive.

Zoom, for instance, has revolutionized virtual communication, offering a range of features that go beyond basic video conferencing. One of its standout tools is breakout rooms, which allow you to divide your audience into smaller groups for focused discussions. This is particularly useful for workshops, collaborative training sessions, or webinars where interaction and audience participation are crucial. Breakout rooms enable you to engage more deeply with your audience, fostering discussions and brainstorming sessions that would otherwise be difficult in a larger group setting. Additionally, Zoom's screen sharing, real-time chat, and polling features can be used seamlessly to keep your audience involved and make your content more interactive.

On the other hand, Microsoft Teams takes integration to the next level by offering flawless synergy with other Microsoft tools. It allows you to share and collaborate on documents in real time, making it ideal for presentations that require live editing or group input. If your presentation involves reviewing documents, creating shared files, or editing slides collaboratively, Teams provides a smooth and efficient workflow. With features like meeting recording, virtual whiteboards, and customisable backgrounds, Teams also makes it easier to maintain a professional and engaging environment throughout the presentation. The platform's ability to integrate seamlessly with Office 365 ensures that your audience can view and collaborate on content without the technical hiccups that sometimes arise from using third-party tools.

Each of these platforms—Zoom and Microsoft Teams—offers distinct advantages depending on your presentation's goals. Zoom is great for creating interactive experiences and managing large audiences, while Teams excels in facilitating real-time collaboration and content sharing. By understanding the unique features of each tool, you can select the one that best meets your needs and allows you to create a dynamic, engaging presentation.

In addition to these features, virtual platforms also offer tools like live captioning, audience Q&A, and chat moderation to ensure accessibility and streamline audience interaction. These features make it easier to cater to a diverse audience, ensuring that everyone has an opportunity to engage with your content.

Incorporating these advanced virtual tools into your presentations not only enhances the delivery of your message but also fosters greater interaction and collaboration with your audience. By mastering the features of these platforms, you can create more immersive, engaging experiences that resonate long after the presentation ends.

To keep virtual audiences engaged, it's important to use tailored strategies. Interactive Q&A sessions can turn a static presentation into a lively discussion. Encourage your audience to ask questions throughout and set aside specific times to address them. This not only keeps them involved but also provides insights into their thoughts. Real-time polling is another effective way to engage your audience. Platforms like Zoom and Microsoft Teams have built-in polling features that allow you to receive instant feedback, making the session more interactive.

However, virtual presentations come with challenges. Internet connectivity issues can disrupt your flow and frustrate both you and your audience. To minimize this risk, use a wired internet connection whenever possible and have a backup plan, like a mobile hotspot. Good audio and visuals are crucial as well. Invest in a quality microphone and camera, and test them before your presentation to ensure everything runs smoothly.

Honestly speaking, building an online presence goes beyond just speaking into a camera; it's about connecting with your audience, even though screens. Making eye contact is still important, so look directly at your camera instead of the screen to create a sense of connection. Additionally, choose a clean, professional background or use a virtual one if your platform allows; this helps maintain focus on your message.

By implementing these strategies, you can effectively engage your virtual audience and make your presentations impactful. Leveraging the features of virtual platforms, using interactive techniques, and overcoming common challenges will help you create a session that resonates with your audience, keeping them connected and involved.

Effective use of Visual Aids

Visual aids are not just supplementary tools in your presentation— they are your secret weapon to cut through a noisy auditorium and ensure your message truly resonates with your audience. Think of visual aids as the perfect tools for a task. Their power lies in understanding their purpose and impact. When chosen and used effectively, they transform your presentation from a monologue into an immersive experience that captures attention and reinforces your key points.

Graphs and charts are among the most powerful visual aids. They help simplify complex data, converting abstract numbers into relatable stories. By visually representing trends, comparisons, and relationships, graphs and charts allow your audience to grasp concepts quickly and easily. Rather than overwhelming your listeners with dense statistics, you give them a visual snapshot that highlights crucial insights. This visual representation makes the information more accessible and memorable, ensuring that your audience walks away with a clearer understanding of your message.

Videos, on the other hand, inject energy and life into your presentation. Whether you're demonstrating a process, showcasing customer testimonials, or bringing in an expert's perspective, videos engage the senses in ways that static visuals cannot. A well-chosen video not only captures attention but also establishes an emotional connection with your audience. It can bring a topic to life, making it relatable and engaging. Integrating videos into your presentation adds variety and dynamism, preventing monotony and ensuring your audience stays focused throughout.

However, simply including visuals is not enough; the true power of visual aids comes from creating clear, impactful, and aesthetically appealing content. High-quality images and graphics can elevate your presentation, making it stand out and capturing the attention of your audience. Whether it's a professional image, an infographic, or a sleek design element, these visuals draw the eye and help emphasize your key points.

Consistency is key when it comes to the design of your visual aids. A unified design—consistent colour schemes, fonts, and layouts—creates a cohesive visual narrative that supports your message. It enhances the professionalism of your presentation and helps the audience stay engaged. Consistent design elements help your visuals feel connected, guiding your audience through your content with ease. When every element feels part of the bigger picture, it becomes easier for the audience to follow along and absorb the information.

While aesthetics matter, clarity is paramount. Avoid visual clutter by ensuring that every element on the screen serves a specific purpose. Each image, graph, and video should enhance your message, not distract from it. Be selective with your visuals—less is often more. Use space strategically to allow your audience to focus on key visuals without feeling overwhelmed by too much information. A clean, well-organised design ensures that your message is communicated effectively without confusion.

In summary, visual aids are much more than just decorations for your presentation—they are powerful tools that enhance understanding, engagement, and retention. By carefully selecting the right visuals, creating cohesive and aesthetically appealing designs, and maintaining clarity, you ensure that your presentation is not only informative but also memorable. When done right, visuals do more than support your speech; they become an integral part of your storytelling, helping your message resonate long after the presentation ends.

More importantly, integrating visual aids beautifully into your presentation involves careful timing and flow. Your visuals should support your words, not overshadow them. Introduce each visual aid at the right moment to reinforce your message without overwhelming the audience. Avoid overcrowding your slides with too much information; a cluttered slide can confuse rather than clarify. Instead, use bullet points or short phrases to highlight key ideas, allowing your visuals to enhance your message and guide your audience through your presentation easily.

Moreover, evaluating the effectiveness of your visual aids is crucial for refining your presentation skills. Gather feedback from your audience to see what worked and what didn't. Did the visuals help clarify their understanding? Were they engaging or distracting? Observing audience reactions—like body language and facial expressions—can reveal how well your visuals resonate. Pay attention to whether people are leaning in, nodding, or appearing confused, and use this feedback to make necessary adjustments.

Finally, by effectively incorporating visual aids, you can transform your presentation from a simple talk into an engaging visual experience. Remember to choose the right aids, design them thoughtfully, integrate them smoothly, and evaluate their impact. These principles will help you create a presentation that not only informs but also transforms and captivates your audience. In the next chapter, we'll discuss how to connect with diverse audiences, ensuring your message resonates across different cultural backgrounds.

Chapter 8:
Addressing Cultural Sensitivity and Inclusivity

In the previous chapter, we discussed how to leverage technology to ensure a smooth, engaging presentation. While technology can enhance your delivery, it's the message itself that truly matters. And in today's globalised world, it's crucial that your message is not only clear but also culturally sensitive and inclusive. A presentation that resonates across diverse audiences requires an understanding of the values, perspectives, and experiences that shape the way people hear and interpret your words.

Addressing cultural sensitivity and inclusivity isn't just about avoiding missteps; it's about creating a space where every audience member feels respected, valued, and understood. Whether you're speaking to a local community or an international audience, recognising cultural nuances and embracing inclusivity will strengthen your connection with your listeners, making your message more powerful and impactful.

In this chapter, you'll learn strategies for cultivating cultural awareness in your speech, from understanding cultural differences to using language that fosters inclusion.

Cultural sensitivity and inclusivity are like navigating a foreign country where you're surrounded by a language you don't understand. At first, the challenge may feel overwhelming, but you quickly realise that communication extends beyond words; it involves gestures, facial expressions, and body language. These non-verbal cues become your tools for connection, helping you understand and engage with the people around you. This experience is a perfect metaphor for public speaking, where recognising and respecting cultural nuances can significantly impact how your message is received and how well you connect with your audience.

Cultural nuances are the subtle differences in behaviour, values, and communication styles that vary from one culture to another. These differences shape how diverse audiences perceive and interpret your words, gestures, and tone. When you identify and respect these nuances, you can adapt your speech to resonate more effectively with your listeners, ensuring that your message is not only heard but understood in the way you intend. Without this awareness, even well-meaning messages can be misinterpreted, leading to misunderstandings or alienation.

Non-verbal cues, in particular, often communicate more than words ever could. For instance, a gesture that symbolizes agreement in one culture may hold an entirely different meaning in another. In some cultures, maintaining direct eye contact is seen as a sign of confidence and honesty, while in others, it may be considered rude or confrontational. Similarly, hand gestures can carry vastly different meanings depending on where you are in the world. A friendly wave or thumbs-up, which are universally recognised in many Western cultures, might be offensive or misunderstood in another region.

For example, in my own culture in Ghana, West Africa, using the left hand to greet someone or to shake hands is considered disrespectful. However, in many Western countries, this action is perfectly acceptable and carries no negative connotations. I also recall a personal experience that taught me the importance of understanding cultural gestures. When I arrived in the UK in 2001,

I tried to get someone's attention by clicking my fingers—something that is

commonly used in Ghana, even in classrooms to signal a teacher for a question. To my surprise, the person responded by saying, "I'm not a dog." While I understood his reaction, it was eye-opening to see how different cultures interpret the same gesture in vastly contrasting ways.

This experience underscored an important lesson: effective communication requires more than just mastering verbal language; it also involves understanding the non-verbal signals that accompany your words. By being attuned to these cultural differences, especially when words may fall short, you can bridge gaps and create a more inclusive and respectful dialogue.

When preparing to speak to a diverse audience, it's crucial to familiarize yourself with their cultural expectations and non-verbal communication styles. For example, in some cultures, silence is a sign of respect and attentiveness, while in others, it's a sign of disinterest or disengagement. Understanding these distinctions helps you avoid misinterpretations and ensures that your message lands in a way that resonates with everyone in the room. This awareness can transform your presentation from a simple exchange of information into a deeper, more meaningful conversation.

Hence cultural sensitivity and inclusivity are not just nice-to-haves; they are essential components of effective communication. Recognising and respecting cultural nuances—both verbal and non-verbal—allows you to connect with your audience on a deeper level. By doing so, you ensure that your message is not only heard but also understood and appreciated, regardless of the audience's background. Through this thoughtful approach, you create a space where everyone feels valued and engaged, fostering a more impactful and inclusive conversation.

Understanding cultural differences in communication is essential when addressing diverse audiences. In high-context cultures, like those in Asia or the Middle East, messages often rely on nuance and the surrounding context. Contrarily, low-context cultures, such as the United States and Germany, value direct and clear messaging, where words carry the primary meaning. Recognising these differences enables you to adjust your communication style, ensuring clarity and reducing misunderstandings.

To prepare effectively for presenting to a culturally diverse audience, research is key. Understanding the cultural contexts of your listeners is essential for creating a presentation that is not only relevant but also respectful. Researching cultural norms, values, and etiquette allows you to tailor your message in a way that resonates deeply with your audience. Cultural guides, articles, and books can be incredibly helpful in providing insights into different customs, communication styles, and expectations. Whether you're exploring the nuances of hierarchy, gift-giving traditions, or family dynamics, these resources offer rich, detailed perspectives on the values that shape your audience's worldview.

In addition to printed materials, engaging with cultural experts, local community members, or consultants can provide invaluable first-hand knowledge. These experts can offer you a nuanced understanding of their specific cultural contexts that books and online articles may not fully capture. They can share experiences, give advice on how to approach sensitive topics, and even help you navigate potential cultural pitfalls. By making this investment in research, you show a deep respect for the backgrounds and perspectives of your audience, which will ultimately help you build rapport and foster stronger connections.

One of the most visible elements of cultural differences in presentations is how people perceive appearance and dress codes. In some cultures, dressing in formal business attire, such as a suit and tie, signals professionalism and respect, whereas in other cultures, a more relaxed, business-casual style is preferred. Recognising and adjusting your attire to align with the expectations of your audience is a small but powerful way to enhance your connection. If you're unsure about the dress code, it's always a good idea to ask your hosts or refer to any guidelines that have been provided. The effort you put into aligning with the local dress customs shows that you value your audience's culture and are willing to adapt to their expectations.

Greeting protocols are another significant cultural consideration. While a handshake is widely recognised as a sign of respect in many cultures, other cultures have different, equally meaningful ways of greeting. In Japan, for instance, a bow is the preferred gesture of respect, whereas in some parts of the Middle East, a slight nod or placing your hand over your heart may be more common. In some African cultures, people may greet with an embrace or a traditional verbal salutation. In cultures where physical touch is not common, a warm smile and respectful words may be sufficient. Taking the time to learn the customary greeting can create an immediate sense of trust and rapport, and it demonstrates your awareness and respect for local customs.

A powerful way to connect with your audience is by making the effort to learn a few words in their language, even if it's just a simple greeting or thank you. This can go a long way in breaking down barriers and showing your audience that you value their culture. You don't need to be fluent—just a few well-chosen words can make a big impact and foster goodwill. For example, learning how to say "hello," "thank you," or "good morning" in the native language of your audience can make your introduction feel more personal, helping to establish an emotional connection. It's important to remember, however, that pronunciation matters—getting it right, or at least making an effort, shows respect for the language and its speakers.

While it's crucial to appreciate the unique cultural traits of your audience, it's equally important to avoid the trap of stereotypes. Cultural stereotypes are oversimplified and often inaccurate generalizations that can diminish the individual identities of the people you're addressing. They can lead to misunderstandings and even offend the very people you're trying to connect with. Instead of reducing an entire group to a set of characteristics, take the time to explore the diversity within that group. Cultures are complex and ever-evolving, and while there may be shared traditions or values, every individual will have their own unique experiences. By resisting the urge to generalize, you create a space for open-mindedness, where every individual feels valued as a person, not just as a representative of their culture.

Encouraging this sense of open-mindedness in your presentation helps foster an environment where diverse perspectives are welcomed. Be mindful of the language you use to ensure that it does not unintentionally alienate or exclude any group. For example, using inclusive language that reflects a global perspective or acknowledging cultural diversity can make your audience feel seen and heard. It's also valuable to encourage audience members to share their perspectives or experiences. This not only enriches the conversation but allows you to learn from the diverse perspectives in the room, which in turn enhances the overall quality of your presentation.

In some cases, cultural differences may arise around topics that are considered taboo or sensitive in certain regions. This could include issues related to politics, religion, gender, or even the role of family and social structures. Researching the cultural sensitivity of these subjects and exercising caution when addressing them is important. You may need to adjust the tone or the way you present these issues to avoid offending or alienating your audience. Being respectful and acknowledging the cultural sensitivities around these topics can prevent misunderstandings and keep the presentation on track.

Additionally, humour is a great tool for connecting with an audience, but it's important to be aware of cultural differences in what is considered funny or appropriate. Jokes that are well-received in one culture may be offensive or misunderstood in another. Using humour with care and awareness can help lighten the mood, but always keep the cultural context in mind.

Ultimately, by taking the time to research and understand the cultural norms of your audience, you position yourself as a thoughtful and considerate speaker. This preparation will not only make your message more likely to resonate but also create a lasting impression of respect, inclusivity, and cultural sensitivity. Each time you present, you have an opportunity to engage with individuals from diverse backgrounds, learn from them, and share your knowledge in a way that's meaningful and respectful. This approach ensures that your message is heard, appreciated, and valued, regardless of the cultural backgrounds of those in your audience.

Thus the cultural sensitivity and inclusivity are not just about avoiding misunderstandings—they're about building genuine connections with your audience. By tailoring your presentation to reflect the cultural nuances of your listeners, you not only make your message more impactful but also foster a greater sense of belonging and respect in the room. As public speakers, it's our responsibility to ensure that everyone feels acknowledged, included, and respected, and this effort begins with thoughtful cultural research and an open mind. When we engage with our audiences on this deeper level, we create an environment where communication flows smoothly and where diverse voices are heard and valued.

8.1 Interactive Element: Cultural Awareness Exercise

Think back to a time when you interacted with someone from a different culture. How did their communication style differ from your own? Were there specific non-verbal cues—like gestures, facial expressions, or body language—that caught your attention? Perhaps their tone of voice, level of eye contact, or personal space boundaries were different than what you're accustomed to. Take a moment to reflect on any cultural surprises or misunderstandings that may have occurred. These moments can be invaluable learning experiences that help you understand the subtleties of intercultural communication.

Consider how you navigated these differences. Did you make adjustments in your approach to ensure your message was clear and respectful? Perhaps you adapted your body language to align with their cultural expectations, or you adjusted your tone to create a more welcoming atmosphere. Maybe you learned a few words in their language to make them feel more comfortable or simply smiled as a way to bridge the gap. Whatever strategies you used, jot down your observations and the adjustments you made. This reflection can offer insights into your strengths and areas for growth in cross-cultural communication.

Think also about how the other person responded. Were they open to your efforts, or did they seem confused or uncomfortable? This can be a signal of how well your communication strategies worked and where you might need to refine your approach. As you reflect on these experiences, ask yourself how you can apply this newfound awareness to future interactions. What have you learned about the importance of cultural sensitivity and how it shapes meaningful communication?

By reflecting on these past interactions, you can build a deeper understanding of cultural differences and enhance your ability to communicate across cultures. Over time, this self-awareness will help you connect more effectively with diverse audiences, fostering an environment of mutual respect and understanding. Use this reflection as a guide for future conversations, and continue to cultivate the skills that make you a more adaptable and empathetic communicator.

8.2 Language and Tone Sensitivity

Language goes beyond mere words; it serves as a bridge that connects us and shapes our interactions. When we speak publicly, using inclusive language is essential. This means choosing words that respect and acknowledge everyone in the audience. For example, opting for "businessperson" instead of "businessman" or "chairperson" instead of "chairman" is a simple yet impactful way to embrace gender diversity and make everyone feel included.

It's also important to use person-first language. Instead of labelling someone by a characteristic, like "disabled person," prefer "person with a disability." This approach highlights their humanity first, rather than defining them by a single trait. Thoughtful language choices create a welcoming environment where everyone feels valued.

Adapting your tone and style to fit cultural contexts is crucial. Different cultures have varying expectations regarding formality. For instance, a formal tone is often appreciated in professional settings in Japan, while a more casual, conversational style might resonate better in the United States. Understanding direct versus indirect communication styles can also influence how your message is received. Direct communication is typically valued in Western cultures, while many Afro-Caribbean and Asian cultures may prefer a more indirect approach that relies on context and implication.

We also have to be cautious with the use of idiomatic expressions and slang, as these can confuse audiences unfamiliar with the phrases. For example, sayings like "kick the bucket" may not translate well and could leave non-native speakers puzzled. It's wise to avoid such expressions or explain them adequately. Ambiguous terms can also cause misunderstandings, so choosing straightforward language and providing context can help ensure clarity.

Gathering feedback and conducting sensitivity checks are invaluable in refining your language and tone. Engaging with people from diverse backgrounds can provide insight into how different audiences may perceive your speech. Consider conducting pre-speech reviews with colleagues or friends from varied cultural perspectives to highlight potential issues. Consulting cross-cultural communication experts can further refine your approach and ensure you communicate with respect and inclusivity.

When preparing for a diverse audience, remember that it's not just about the words you say; it's also about how you say them. By thoughtfully selecting your language and adjusting your style to fit different cultural contexts, you can foster deeper connections and more meaningful communication.

8.3 Delivering Globally Resonant Speeches

Adapting your speech for a global audience is like standing before a diverse group of individuals, each shaped by distinct cultures, histories, and personal experiences. In such a setting, it's crucial to transcend cultural boundaries and speak to the heart of what unites us all. A powerful way to do this is by focusing on universal themes such as hope, perseverance, love, and unity. These are values that resonate deeply with people, regardless of their background, language, or belief system. By emphasizing these timeless principles, you can connect with your audience on a profound, emotional level that transcends geographical and cultural differences.

To truly enhance the relevance and appeal of your message, it's important to weave in global perspectives. Rather than limiting yourself to local examples, draw from a wide range of stories, case studies, and experiences from around the world. Share how various cultures approach similar challenges and showcase solutions that have proven successful across different contexts. For example, you might highlight a grassroots initiative in Africa that uses community-based health care to combat disease, or discuss how businesses in Asia have incorporated sustainable practices to address environmental concerns. By broadening your examples, you not only make your speech more relatable to a wider audience but also demonstrate a deep respect for the rich diversity of global experiences.

In addition to content, the logistics of addressing an international audience require thoughtful consideration. Time zones, for example, play a significant role in scheduling and can affect participation. When organising virtual presentations or global conferences, be mindful of the best time for the majority of your audience, even if it means adjusting your own schedule. This shows that you value their participation and are considerate of their time.

Language differences also need to be addressed. If you're speaking to an audience that spans multiple countries, consider offering translations or subtitles to make your presentation more accessible. Even when your audience speaks the same language, providing translations can help them feel more comfortable, ensuring that your message is conveyed clearly and inclusively. This attention to detail fosters a sense of belonging and respect, which is essential for building a connection with your audience.

As discussed previously, technology is a vital tool for bridging the gap between you and your global audience. With platforms like Zoom, Microsoft Teams, and other video conferencing tools, you can reach people across the world. These platforms offer features like breakout rooms, polls, and live chats that allow for real-time engagement and interaction, making your speech feel more dynamic and participatory. Furthermore, translation software and AI-driven language tools can facilitate communication with non-native speakers, breaking down language barriers and enabling more meaningful connections.

Take inspiration from successful speakers who have mastered the art of adapting their messages for global audiences. Figures like Les Brown, the late Jim Rohn, Tony Robbins, Andy Harrington, and others have built their careers by understanding the nuances of diverse audiences and tailoring their messages accordingly. At international conferences, these speakers skilfully navigate cultural differences by using universal themes in their stories and incorporating visuals that resonate across borders. For instance, at a global health summit, a speaker might present case studies from various countries, illustrating the global impact of a new health initiative. This approach not only broadens the impact of their message but also inspires collective action across cultural and national boundaries.

Similarly, in the corporate world, leaders who present to international markets often customise their pitches to align with the values and expectations of foreign markets. They take the time to understand the cultural context of their audience, adapting their tone, messaging, and even product offerings to demonstrate respect for local customs while emphasizing the universal benefits of their products or services. This shows that, while the core message remains the same, thoughtful adaptation ensures that it resonates with the unique needs and preferences of each audience.

In essence, adapting your speech for a global audience is about being mindful of cultural differences while focusing on what unites us all. By incorporating universal themes, showcasing global perspectives, and leveraging technology to engage audiences across distances, you can create presentations that are both meaningful and impactful. The most successful global communicators understand that it's not just about sharing information—it's about fostering understanding, building connections, and inspiring action on a global scale.

Interactive Element: Global Audience Checklist

When preparing for an upcoming presentation, it's essential to tailor it for a global audience. To ensure your message resonates with people from various cultural backgrounds and locations, here's a simple checklist to guide you in making your presentation more inclusive and effective:

Identify Universal Themes

Focus on topics that have universal appeal, such as innovation, teamwork, resilience, and personal growth. These are values that transcend cultural, geographical, and linguistic differences, making it easier for your audience to connect with your message on a deeper level.

Include Global Perspectives

Enrich your presentation by sharing examples, stories, and case studies from different countries. This not only broadens the scope of your message but also demonstrates your awareness and respect for diverse experiences. By including global perspectives, you show that you understand the world is multifaceted and that your message applies beyond local contexts.

Consider Time Zones

One of the key logistical challenges of presenting to a global audience is time zones. When scheduling your presentation, select a time that is convenient for the majority of attendees, or at least ensures that those in major regions can participate. If it's not feasible to accommodate everyone, consider recording the presentation and providing it on-demand for those who can't attend live.

Provide Translations or Subtitles

To ensure your message is understood by everyone, offering translations or subtitles in multiple languages can be a game-changer. This is particularly important for non-native speakers, as it enhances accessibility and allows for a smoother communication process. Even when speaking in a shared language like English, subtitles can provide clarity and improve comprehension.

Utilise Technology

Leverage digital tools and platforms to engage your audience effectively. Platforms like Zoom, Microsoft Teams, and Loom provide interactive features like chat, polls, and screen sharing that can increase audience involvement. Additionally, consider using translation services or real-time captioning to assist with language barriers. These tools can bridge communication gaps and ensure your audience feels involved and included, no matter where they are.

By thoughtfully incorporating these elements, you can create a presentation that is not only informative but also inclusive and impactful for a diverse global audience. This approach shows that you value inclusivity and are committed to connecting with people from all walks of life.

8.4 Build Bridges Through Inclusivity

To create a more inclusive environment in public speaking is like inviting everyone to a table where all voices matter. It's about making sure every audience member feels they belong, no matter their background. One effective way to achieve this is by encouraging diverse participation. Invite questions and comments from a variety of perspectives, allowing everyone a chance to contribute. This not only enriches the discussion but also provides a fuller understanding of the topic.

Again, integrating inclusive visuals is also key. Use images and stories that reflect the diversity of your audience, so everyone sees themselves represented. This shows respect and helps build a connection between you and your audience, reinforcing the idea that their experiences are valued.

Moreover, collaboration is another powerful approach. By working with individuals from diverse backgrounds, you can add a wealth of insights to your presentation. Organising panel discussions with multicultural experts can create a richer dialogue and deeper understanding. Joint presentations with international partners also allow for valuable cross-cultural exchange, showcasing different ideas and perspectives.

Fostering open dialogue is essential for inclusivity. Encourage Q&A sessions where diverse voices are celebrated, and create an atmosphere where audience members feel safe sharing their experiences. Hosting cultural exchange workshops can further enhance this understanding, breaking down barriers and building connections within the community.

Finally, commitment to continuous learning is crucial. Cultivating cultural sensitivity is an ongoing process. Attend cultural sensitivity training to gain tools for navigating complex dynamics, and seek cross-cultural networking opportunities to deepen your understanding of different perspectives.

By fusing these strategies into your public speaking will help you build bridges with your audience, creating an environment of respect and understanding. Embracing inclusivity enriches your presentations and strengthens both personal and professional relationships, allowing you to connect more effectively and inspire your audience. In the next chapter we will be exploring the importance of Networking and Personal Branding.

Chapter 9:
Networking and Personal Branding through Public Speaking

In the previous chapter, we focused on the importance of addressing cultural sensitivity and inclusivity, ensuring that your message resonates with diverse audiences in a respectful and meaningful way. But public speaking isn't just about delivering a message—it's also about creating connections and building your personal brand. The way you present yourself, your ideas, and your expertise can open doors to new opportunities and lasting relationships.

Networking and personal branding are powerful outcomes of effective public speaking. Every time you step in front of an audience, you have the chance to establish yourself as a thought leader, build credibility, and expand your professional network. But it takes more than just speaking well; it requires intentionality. You need to position yourself as someone people want to connect with, collaborate with, and learn from.

In this chapter, we'll explore how to use public speaking as a tool for networking and building your personal brand. From crafting an authentic narrative about your journey to strategically engaging with your audience, you'll learn how to leverage every speaking opportunity to expand your influence and cultivate meaningful professional relationships.

In a world full of voices, your brand helps you stand out. It's a mix of your skills, experiences, and values that sets you apart. Think of crafting a personal brand as creating a self-portrait that reflects who you are and connects with your audience.

Public speaking plays a crucial role in this journey. It allows you to share your story and engage authentically with others. To build a strong personal brand, start by identifying your unique value proposition – the skills and qualities that make you different. You can use self-assessment tools like personality tests or skills inventories to discover what you excel at. Reflect on your experiences and the feedback from peers or mentors to gain insights into your strengths.

With this information, craft a personal brand statement that summarizes who you are, what you do, and how you make a difference. A powerful statement is clear, unique, and passionate, highlighting your values and what you bring to the table.

Next, align your brand with your core values. Identify the principles that guide you and what you stand for; these will form the foundation of your brand. By weaving your values into your messaging, you ensure your brand remains authentic and resonates with others, fostering trust and connection. Consistency is key— whether in your speeches, social media posts, or daily interactions, maintaining a cohesive message makes your brand memorable.

Again creating a consistent image across platforms is vital for recognition. Consider designing a personal logo that embodies your identity. A well-crafted logo makes your brand instantly recognisable. Ensure your social media profiles reflect your brand's voice and values with similar language, tone, and imagery, reinforcing your credibility.

More importantly, storytelling is another powerful tool for enhancing your brand. Develop a personal origin story that highlights your journey and the experiences that have shaped you.

This narrative sheds light on your motivations and values, helping others connect with you. Sharing success stories and testimonials adds depth and credibility to your brand, making it relatable and memorable. Through storytelling, you engage your audience and build emotional connections that strengthen your personal brand.

9.1 Interactive Element: Personal Brand Reflection Exercise

Take a moment to reflect on your brand by considering these key questions:

1. Unique Value Proposition: What skills and qualities set you apart? How do they make you unique?

2. Core Values: What are your guiding principles? How do they shape your actions and decisions?

3. Brand Image: How do you present yourself across various platforms? Is your messaging consistent and aligned with your values?

4. Storytelling: What personal stories showcase your journey and achievements? How can you share these stories to connect with your audience?

By reflecting on these elements, you can create a genuine and impactful personal brand.

9.2 Leveraging Networking Opportunities

In public speaking, networking is essential for growing and sustaining your career. The first step is to identify key networking events that can help you build meaningful connections. Industry conferences and seminars are some of the best places to network, as they gather professionals with shared interests and goals. These events provide opportunities for collaboration and learning, allowing you to share your insights and engage with others who can offer valuable new perspectives. Choose conferences that resonate with your expertise to ensure your connections are relevant and beneficial.

Networking mixers and meetups offer a more relaxed atmosphere for connecting with a diverse group of people. These informal settings encourage open conversations, where you can discuss ideas and explore potential collaborations. By participating actively—whether by asking questions or sharing your experiences—you enhance your visibility and establish your presence in the field.

Engaging with influencers requires a thoughtful approach. Influencers can significantly impact your career, so building relationships with them is beneficial. Personalise your outreach by reflecting genuine interest in their work. Highlight common interests and express how their insights have influenced you. This sincerity increases the chances of a positive response. Additionally, think about how you can add value to their work—through collaboration, sharing resources, or unique insights. This mutual benefit can lead to fruitful partnerships.

Also public speaking engagements themselves also serve as excellent networking opportunities. Hosting workshops or panels allows you to showcase your expertise and engage directly with your audience. These interactions position you as a thought leader while connecting you with potential collaborators or clients. Events like seminars and training sessions offer similar chances to impart valuable knowledge and expand your professional circle.

To cultivate your network through audience engagement, take the time to interact with attendees after your presentation. Collecting business cards or contact information helps maintain those connections. Following up with personalised messages is key to solidifying these relationships. Express gratitude for their attendance and reference specific points from your conversation to show genuine interest. This thoughtful follow-up makes you memorable and increases the likelihood of further interactions. By nurturing these connections, you enrich your career with diverse perspectives and opportunities.

9.3 Create Lasting Impressions

To Step into a room full of strangers can feel daunting, but see it as an opportunity to create connections. Crafting a memorable introduction is like painting on a blank canvas. Your elevator pitch acts as your brush—a concise yet powerful summary that captures who you are and what you bring to the table. Think about it as your verbal business card, designed to leave a lasting impression long after you've parted ways.

Your pitch should be clear and adaptable, fitting different audiences while staying true to your core message. And adding a touch of humour or a relatable anecdote can lighten the mood and turn a formal introduction into a friendly conversation. When used wisely, humour eases any tension, and personal stories invite others to engage and relate to your experiences.

To create positive impressions, authenticity and confidence are essential. Maintain eye contact to show attentiveness and respect, which helps foster trust. Positive body language—like an open stance, relaxed shoulders, and a warm smile—further communicates your confidence and approachability. As you interact, share your personal insights. Let your passion and sincerity shine through, providing a glimpse into what shapes your perspective. Such authenticity resonates with others, paving the way for meaningful connections.

Active listening is another key element of memorable interactions that creates lasting impression. It's not just about hearing but genuinely valuing the speaker's message. By paraphrasing and reflecting on their points, you show engagement and investment in the conversation. Thoughtful follow-up questions also invite deeper discussions, allowing the conversation to grow. Through active listening, you build rapport and trust, creating connections that go beyond the surface level.

Lastly, commit to continuous improvement in your networking and public speaking skills which is vital for long-term success. When you seek feedback, whether through post-event surveys or insights from peers and mentors, can help you see how your message is received and identify areas for growth. Moreover, to embrace feedback fosters a cycle of learning, ensuring that each interaction improves upon the last. This dedication to growth not only enhances your skills but also demonstrates your openness and commitment to excellence, allowing you to leave impactful impressions wherever you go.

9.4 Build Authority and Influence

To build authority and influence in public speaking is like being at the forefront of your industry, where your insights and expertise resonate beyond your immediate circle. To establish yourself as a thought leader through public speaking is a powerful way to achieve this. It all starts with sharing your knowledge widely. By publishing articles or white papers, you can articulate your ideas and provide valuable content that reaches a broader audience. These publications highlight your expertise and establish you as a reliable source of information in your field.

In order to succeed, choose topics that tackle current challenges or innovations which enhances your credibility and help you stand out as an expert. Speaking at prominent industry events is another key way to amplify your presence. These platforms allow you to engage with peers and leaders, share your vision, and contribute meaningfully to discussions in your area of expertise. Visibility at such events solidifies your status as a thought leader and opens doors to new connections and opportunities.

It is also absolutely important to build a portfolio of speaking engagements showcases your accomplishments. Document each engagement, note the audience size, event significance, and the impact of your presentation. This record becomes tangible evidence of your experience and effectiveness as a speaker. Create an online speaker profile that can also boost your visibility and include highlights from your engagements, testimonials from attendees, and any media coverage you've received. By showcasing your experience online, you make it easier for event organisers to discover you, increasing your chances of being invited to speak at prestigious events.

Moreover, leveraging media and publicity can further enhance your authority. Reach out to industry publications with well-crafted pitches to gain media attention. These outlets seek fresh perspectives and expert insights to engage their audience. Your contributions—whether interviews, guest articles, or opinion pieces—can establish you as a go-to expert in your field. Podcasts or webinars participation is another great way to share your knowledge and reach new audiences in an accessible format. Engaging with the media expands your reach and reinforces your reputation as a respected thought leader.

Continuous learning and adaptation helps you sustain your influence because the landscape of any field is ever-changing, so staying informed about emerging trends is crucial for maintaining relevance. Attending professional development courses enhances your knowledge and skills, providing fresh insights that can inform your work. By staying ahead of the curve, you demonstrate your commitment to excellence and inspire others to seek your guidance.

In summary, this chapter explored how building authority and influence through public speaking can elevate your professional profile. By positioning yourself as a thought leader, documenting your speaking engagements, leveraging media, and committing to continuous learning, you can make a lasting impact in your field. This foundation sets the stage for further growth and opportunities, leading us to the next chapter's focus on transforming feedback into long-term growth and mastery in public speaking.

Chapter 10:
Transformative Practice and Feedback

In the previous chapter, we explored how to use public speaking as a tool for networking and personal branding, turning every speaking opportunity into a chance to build connections and elevate your professional presence. But to truly make an impact, it's essential to focus on the process that leads up to those opportunities: the practice and feedback that shape you into a stronger, more confident speaker.

No one becomes a powerful speaker overnight. The key to long-term success lies in consistent practice and embracing constructive feedback. This is where true transformation occurs. By practicing regularly, you refine your delivery, strengthen your content, and gain greater self-awareness. And feedback—whether from peers, mentors, or your own observations—provides the insights you need to continually grow and improve.

This chapter is designed to help you discover the most effective opportunities for improving your public speaking abilities, whether through local clubs, online platforms, or personal setups. Each of these avenues offers unique advantages, providing distinct ways to hone your skills and gain confidence in your speaking abilities. Whether you're just beginning or looking to refine your expertise, these resources will help guide you on your journey to becoming a more compelling speaker.

10.1 Ways to Improve Your Public Speaking Skills

One of the easiest and most effective ways to enhance your public speaking skills is by joining local speaking clubs. Organisations like Toastmasters International are renowned for providing a supportive, structured environment where you can practice and improve. Toastmasters clubs are located all around the world, making it easy to find one that fits your schedule and geographical location. These clubs operate on a membership-based structure that encourages regular practice and provides opportunities to speak in front of an audience.

Toastmasters offers an invaluable community where members engage in a variety of speaking exercises. Whether delivering prepared speeches, impromptu talks, or participating in group discussions, members gain the chance to speak often in a constructive, low-stakes environment. Additionally, clubs regularly host Speak-a-thons, Speech Contests, and other events that give you the opportunity to showcase your skills in front of a larger audience.

The real benefit of Toastmasters and similar organisations is the community of like-minded individuals who are also committed to self-improvement. This creates a safe space where you can experiment with different speaking styles, test new techniques, and receive feedback that helps you grow. The friendships formed in these settings often become a source of encouragement and inspiration, allowing you to overcome nervousness and continue pushing yourself.

Similarly, joining a community debate group or discussion club can be an excellent opportunity to practice your speaking skills in a different setting. In these groups, you'll be challenged to think on your feet, organise your thoughts quickly, and articulate your opinions under pressure. Engaging in these types of discussions helps you become more agile in your speaking abilities and boosts your confidence when addressing any kind of audience.

Embrace Online Platforms and Technology

In addition to traditional face-to-face groups, the digital age has opened up exciting new opportunities for improving your public speaking skills. Virtual reality (VR) training programs such as VirtualSpeech and Ovation VR simulate real-life speaking environments, allowing you to practice speeches in realistic scenarios. Whether you're preparing for a wedding toast, an investor pitch, or any other speaking engagement, these platforms immerse you in different settings and provide real-time feedback on your speech patterns, body language, pacing, and gestures.

The advantage of VR is that it allows you to practice your speeches in a controlled environment where you can simulate various situations without the pressure of a live audience. These tools give you the flexibility to practice at your own pace and make adjustments based on the feedback you receive, all from the comfort of your home. It's an excellent option for people who prefer a more tech-driven, personalised approach to their development.

Furthermore, online public speaking meetups are another fantastic resource for connecting with speakers from around the world. These virtual gatherings bring together diverse groups of people, providing an opportunity for global networking and exchanging insights with speakers of different backgrounds and cultures. Practicing in such a setting exposes you to various speaking styles, allowing you to adapt your approach and refine your delivery for diverse audiences.

Create a Personal Practice Space

In addition to joining formal groups or using online tools, setting up a personal practice space can significantly boost your confidence and progress. One of the best investments you can make in your growth as a public speaker is creating a home environment where you can regularly rehearse, record, and review your speeches. A home recording studio doesn't need to be fancy or expensive. It simply requires a quiet space with a good camera and microphone so you can film your speeches and watch them back.

Recording your practice sessions is invaluable because it allows you to see yourself from an audience's perspective. By analysing your body language, gestures, vocal modulation, and facial expressions, you can gain a deeper understanding of your strengths and areas for improvement. Watching these recordings will also help you become more comfortable with the sound of your own voice, ultimately leading to a more natural and confident delivery.

Simulated audience practice is another powerful tool in your personal practice setup. Gather family members, friends, or colleagues who are willing to sit through your rehearsals and provide feedback. Their insights can help you identify any distractions, areas that need more clarity, or moments when your delivery may not have the desired impact. These personal sessions also give you the opportunity to practice engaging with a live audience, helping you build confidence and refine your performance before a larger crowd.

Participate in Public Speaking Workshops

For those looking to take their skills to the next level, public speaking workshops offer structured environments for guided practice and expert feedback. These workshops provide intensive, hands-on training that covers a wide range of topics, including speech structure, vocal delivery, visual aids, and audience engagement—skills that are covered in more depth throughout this book.

Weekend intensive workshops or seminars are ideal for individuals looking to immerse themselves in public speaking without the long-term commitment of a club or ongoing program. These sessions focus on actionable skills, providing you with immediate feedback that you can use to improve your next speaking engagement. Through these workshops, you'll gain access to expert facilitators who offer personalised insights and give you specific tools for overcoming your speaking challenges.

For those with more specialized needs, speech coaching sessions can provide one-on-one support. A personalised coaching approach allows you to work on specific aspects of your speaking, whether it's overcoming stage fright, mastering a persuasive pitch, or perfecting your delivery style. Coaches provide targeted feedback that is tailored to your unique strengths and challenges, helping you refine your speaking style and achieve your public speaking goals faster.

Blend Theory with Practice for Continuous Growth

The key to ongoing success in public speaking is blending theory with practice. Whether you're learning techniques from books and workshops or refining your skills through personal continuously challenging yourself, seeking new opportunities for practice, and staying engaged with learning materials, you can create a personal development plan that evolves with your speaking journey.

Interactive Element: Practice Opportunities Checklist

Find Local Clubs

The first step to improving your public speaking is to find a local community where you can practice and grow. Toastmasters International is one of the most recognised global organisations, offering a welcoming environment where you can practice public speaking regularly. Toastmasters clubs are located worldwide, and by attending their meetings, you'll not only practice speaking but also receive constructive feedback from fellow members, helping you develop your skills at your own pace. In addition, community debate groups can be an excellent way to enhance your ability to think on your feet and communicate effectively under pressure. The diverse group of people in these settings can offer different perspectives, fostering your personal growth.

Use Online Tools

In today's digital world, you don't need to rely solely on in-person practice. Online tools, especially Virtual Reality (VR) platforms, can offer an immersive and flexible way to practice public speaking. Programs like VirtualSpeech simulate real-life speaking environments, such as boardrooms, weddings, or public presentations, enabling you to practice without leaving your home. These tools provide instant feedback on your delivery, helping you adjust your tone, body language, pacing, and overall presence. They are especially valuable for introverts or those who want to rehearse in private before stepping in front of a live audience.

Create Your Space

Sometimes, the best practice happens in your own space. Setting up a home recording studio doesn't require a lot of investment—just a quiet room, a camera, and a microphone. Recording your speeches allows you to watch yourself from the audience's perspective, giving you insights into your body language, gestures, and voice modulation. In addition, you can gather family or friends to act as your simulated audience. Their feedback—whether it's about your clarity, engagement, or timing—will help you improve your performance and ensure that you're ready for any crowd, big or small.

Join Workshops

For a more structured approach, workshops and coaching sessions are invaluable. Sign up for public speaking workshops where you'll get focused training and personalised feedback from experienced coaches. Whether it's an intensive weekend seminar or a series of smaller, specialized sessions, workshops allow you to sharpen specific skills, such as voice projection, speech structuring, or managing stage fright. Working with a coach can help you identify your strengths and areas for improvement, ensuring that your speaking style continues to evolve.

Incorporating These Practices into Your Routine

By integrating these various practice methods into your routine— whether through local clubs, online tools, personal practice spaces, or expert coaching—you can transform public speaking from a daunting task into a confident, engaging experience. Over time, you'll gain a deeper understanding of your style, refine your delivery, and ultimately become a more impactful and effective speaker. Each step, no matter how small, will contribute to your ongoing growth as a communicator, building the confidence needed to inspire and captivate any audience.

10.2 Utilise Feedback for Growth

Feedback serves as a valuable tool for identifying both your strengths and areas for improvement. Constructive criticism can greatly enhance your public speaking skills, allowing you to focus on weaknesses and turn them into strengths. Positive feedback builds confidence, enabling you to build upon what you do well. This awareness of both your strengths and weaknesses fosters personal growth. Instead of fearing criticism, welcoming it as an opportunity can transform each speaking engagement into a chance to improve.

To truly unlock the benefits, it's vital to gather feedback from a diverse range of sources. This approach ensures that we capture a full spectrum of insights! Audience surveys after your presentations can provide insight into how your message was received, helping you pinpoint specific areas to enhance.

By tailoring your questions to prioritise clarity, engagement, and relevance, you unlock a powerful tool for understanding your audience. This method not only enhances communication but also fosters a genuine connection, leading to more meaningful interactions and insights. Additionally, seeking advice from professional speech coaches can shed light on technical aspects of your delivery. Their expertise can identify subtle details in your performance that you might overlook, guiding you toward greater skill.

Again how to effectively interpret feedback is vital to gain meaningful insights. It's important to separate personal opinions from objective observations. Subjective feedback may reflect personal tastes, while objective feedback offers measurable aspects of your delivery. For instance, comments on your energy level provide insights into audience engagement, while notes on pacing or volume give clear areas to address. By focusing on these actionable insights, you can prioritise the most impactful changes for your next performance.

Furthermore, set specific, measurable goals based on feedback which is key to turning insights into actionable steps. Create an action plan that outlines manageable goals for improvement. For instance, if feedback suggests enhancing vocal variety, your goal could be to practice differing pitch and tone during rehearsals. Keeping track of your progress helps maintain focus and celebrates small wins, ensuring a steady journey of improvement in your public speaking skills.

Interactive Element: Feedback Reflection Exercise

1.   After your next speaking engagement, gather feedback from at least three people.

2.   Reflect on their comments, look for common themes and unique insights.

3.   Distinguish between subjective and objective feedback, and identify specific areas for improvement.

4.   Use this reflection to set one clear goal for your next presentation and create an action plan to achieve it. By doing this, you'll turn feedback into a powerful tool for your growth as a speaker, helping you become more competent and confident over time.

10.3 The Role of Peer Reviews

As you stand on the stage, feel the warmth of the spotlight illuminating your face. This moment is yours. Let your heart race with excitement—it's a powerful sign that you are ready to command your audience's attention. Harness that energy and step forward with confidence, knowing that you possess the power to captivate and inspire. You've spent countless hours mastering your speech, rehearsing every word, every pause, and every gesture. Yet, there is one element that can truly elevate your performance: feedback.

Feedback from peers who understand the nuances of public speaking can provide invaluable insight, offering perspectives you might have missed or overlooked. They bring fresh eyes to your delivery, helping you refine your approach and deepen your connection with your audience. More importantly, engaging in peer feedback isn't just about pointing out mistakes; it's about creating a community of support where everyone encourages one another, celebrates each other's achievements, and gently steers each other toward improvement. The value of peer reviews lies in the shared learning that fosters growth, making you better equipped for every stage you stand upon.

Growth happens when you surround yourself with individuals who are equally dedicated to enhancing their speaking skills. Building a peer review group creates a nurturing environment where feedback is not only welcome but actively sought. This group becomes a safe space for everyone to develop their skills, share knowledge, and grow together.

Begin by bringing together a group of like-minded people who are committed to improving their public speaking. Set up regular sessions to ensure consistency and momentum. Establish clear expectations and guidelines to ensure that each session is productive and respectful. For example, you could create a simple format where each member presents a speech, followed by feedback from the group. This structure promotes active participation and ensures that everyone has a chance to contribute and learn.

For a peer review group to be truly effective, it's crucial to create an atmosphere of trust and openness. When members feel safe to share their thoughts, they will be more inclined to offer honest, constructive feedback. This environment of support allows for deeper self-reflection, as you know your peers have your best interests at heart.

In such a setting, feedback isn't just a one-way street. Each member of the group should feel valued, both as a speaker and as a contributor. The group can become more than just a space for critique—it evolves into a community where everyone is invested in each other's success. This camaraderie extends beyond the reviews, creating a network of support that will continue to encourage you long after your sessions have ended.

When offering feedback, specificity is key. Rather than simply saying, "That was great!" or "You need to work on that," provide detailed observations that can help the speaker improve. For example, instead of generic praise, you might say, "Your point about X was clear and well-articulated, but perhaps you could emphasize the key takeaway more by slowing down and pausing for effect." This type of feedback helps speakers understand exactly what worked well and what might need tweaking.

Equally important is balancing positive reinforcement with constructive criticism. Recognising the effort put into the speech, even when there are areas that need work, boosts the speaker's confidence and encourages continued growth. Acknowledge the strengths in their delivery, while gently guiding them toward areas for improvement. By doing so, you'll foster an environment of encouragement, which is crucial for long-term progress.

Feedback from peers can be incredibly valuable before you even step onto the stage. During the preparation process, their insights can spark new ideas and boost your confidence.

Experimenting with their suggestions during practice sessions allows you to expand your range and find what resonates most with you and your audience. This experimentation is key, as it helps you discover what works best and what feels most authentic. Peer reviews open the door for you to test new techniques and refine your delivery. The feedback you receive will help you tweak your approach until you find the right balance between what works for you and what will most effectively engage your audience.

Cultivating a long-term network of support is very effective. The benefits of peer reviews go far beyond the immediate feedback you receive. They foster a network of support that can last long after the review session ends. The relationships built through peer reviews become lasting connections that can offer continued guidance and motivation. Whether it's through informal check-ins or ongoing encouragement, the bonds you create within your review group can become invaluable assets in your public speaking journey.

This network isn't just for professional advancement; it's also a space to form friendships and collaborations that transcend public speaking. As you continue to grow, you'll find that these relationships provide a source of inspiration, support, and shared knowledge. In the long run, peer reviews not only help you refine your skills but also build a sense of community that is essential for continuous growth.

By engaging in peer review, you create an ongoing cycle of improvement—one that doesn't just focus on the immediate task at hand but nurtures your growth as a speaker over time. The feedback you receive helps you identify blind spots, celebrate your successes, and continue refining your skills.

More than that, participating in a peer review group pushes you to be open-minded, humble, and willing to explore new ideas. Every session becomes a step forward in your journey to becoming a more confident, effective, and dynamic public speaker.

As you embrace the feedback from your peers, you'll discover that the true power of public speaking doesn't just lie in your performance—it lies in the shared experiences and collective growth that come from a community working together to inspire, challenge, and elevate each other. By transforming your speaking abilities through peer review, you'll not only enhance your craft but also become part of a network of individuals committed to continuous improvement. This journey of growth and collaboration will take you further than you could ever go alone.

10.4 Continuous Improvement Techniques

Creating a Personal Continuous Improvement Plan for public speaking is like mapping out a journey—it provides clear direction, purpose, and focus. Whether you're a seasoned speaker or just starting, having a structured approach to growth is essential to ensure progress. Here's a detailed framework to help you craft your own plan:

1. Set Long-Term and Short-Term Goals

Start by establishing both long-term and short-term goals. Long-term goals might include becoming a keynote speaker at a major conference, mastering persuasive speaking techniques, or delivering impactful TED Talks. These goals give you a clear vision of where you want to be in the future and help you stay motivated.

On the other hand, short-term goals focus on immediate areas of improvement, like enhancing your vocal clarity, managing stage fright, or improving your delivery when speaking in smaller settings, like community groups or workshops. Short-term goals act as milestones, providing quick wins and helping you track incremental progress.

2. Identify Key Areas for Growth

To progress in your public speaking journey, it's important to regularly evaluate your strengths and weaknesses. Reflect on your delivery and audience interaction. Do you struggle with pacing or articulation? Do you feel confident speaking in front of large crowds? Identify these gaps and prioritise the skills that will have the biggest impact on your overall speaking abilities. Some key areas to focus on include:

• **Vocal delivery** (tone, clarity, pacing)

• **Non-verbal communication** (body language, gestures, eye contact)

• **Content structure** (clarity, storytelling, audience engagement)

• **Confidence and presence** (overcoming nerves, stage presence)

Tailor your improvement efforts based on your personal challenges, making each practice session purposeful.

3. Leverage Technology to Enhance Your Practice

In the modern world, technology can significantly elevate your public speaking skills. Use advanced tools to analyse and enhance your delivery:

- **Speech Analysis Software:** These tools provide valuable insights into speech patterns, pacing, volume, and clarity. They give you objective feedback, helping you recognise areas you might overlook during self-reflection.

- **Voice and Diction Apps:** Apps designed to refine pronunciation and articulation are perfect for enhancing vocal clarity. Many of these apps provide customised exercises based on your unique needs, helping you practice at your own pace.

By incorporating these tools into your daily routine, you can pinpoint specific areas for improvement and fine-tune your delivery for maximum impact.

4. Regular Self-Evaluation for Continuous Improvement

Self-evaluation is key to refining your skills. Regularly recording your speeches or presentations allows you to see yourself from the audience's perspective. Pay attention to aspects like:

- **Body language** (gestures, posture, movement)

- **Facial expressions** (engagement, enthusiasm)

- **Vocal delivery** (clarity, tone, speed)

Viewing your recorded speeches will help you spot unconscious habits or tics that might detract from your message. By adjusting these behaviours, you can ensure you're presenting in the most effective way possible.

Additionally, using self-assessment checklists after each practice session allows you to evaluate your performance on key factors such as engagement, pacing, volume, and clarity. This routine provides a structured way to monitor your progress and pinpoint areas for further improvement.

5. Stay Up-to-Date with Public Speaking Trends

Public speaking is a dynamic field that is always evolving. To remain relevant and effective, stay informed about the latest trends and techniques in communication. Attend webinars, conferences, and workshops led by industry leaders to learn about new approaches in public speaking, such as storytelling techniques, audience engagement strategies, and the integration of technology like AI in presentations.

Additionally, subscribe to public speaking journals and read articles about best practices, emerging trends, and innovations in the field. This continual learning will provide you with fresh perspectives and help you adapt your approach as new methods and technologies become available.

6. Celebrate Milestones and Track Your Progress

Improvement is a long-term process, but celebrating small victories along the way helps maintain motivation. Track your achievements—whether it's delivering a speech with newfound confidence, receiving positive feedback from an audience, or overcoming a long-standing fear. These milestones reflect your growth and remind you that progress is being made.

Don't forget to reflect on your journey regularly. Ask yourself questions like:

• What have I learned recently that improved my speaking skills?

• How has my confidence level increased over time?

• What new challenges have I successfully tackled?

Each step, no matter how small, brings you closer to mastering public speaking.

Chapter 11:
How to Adapt to Unexpected Challenges

Prepare and Manage Q and A like a Pro

In the previous chapter, we delved into the transformative power of practice and feedback, which are essential for refining your skills and evolving as a speaker. However, even with all the preparation and practice in the world, one thing is certain: unexpected challenges will arise. Whether it's a technical glitch, an unruly audience, or a sudden change in the event schedule, the ability to adapt and maintain composure in the face of the unexpected is a hallmark of a truly skilled speaker.

Adapting to these challenges isn't about avoiding mistakes—it's about handling them gracefully when they happen. Every speaker will encounter a situation that doesn't go according to plan. The real test is how you respond. With the right strategies, you can turn unforeseen obstacles into opportunities to demonstrate poise, resilience, and quick thinking.

In this chapter, we'll explore practical techniques for staying adaptable under pressure. You'll learn how to troubleshoot problems on the fly, manage disruptions with confidence, and use your communication skills to regain control of the situation. Because when you embrace challenges as part of the experience, you not only handle them—you thrive in them.

When you're on stage, the spotlight shines brightly on you. You've just delivered a powerful conclusion that captivates the audience. As the applause fades, a new phase of your presentation begins: the question-and-answer session. This moment is thrilling, sometimes daunting, and always full of opportunity. Now, you're not just presenting—you're engaging in a dialogue that reveals your depth, adaptability, and poise.

A well-managed Q&A session can significantly boost your credibility and enhance the impact of your presentation. It's a chance to go beyond your prepared content, connect more personally with your audience, and demonstrate your ability to think on your feet.

The secret lies in proactive preparation. Before your presentation, take time to identify areas in your content that may spark curiosity, raise doubts, or invite deeper exploration. Consider your audience— what are their interests, professional backgrounds, or potential pain points? Understanding who's in the room will help you anticipate the types of questions they're most likely to ask.

Crafting clear, informative answers to anticipated questions is a vital part of reinforcing your credibility as a speaker. Your responses should be well thought out—substantial enough to demonstrate your expertise, yet concise enough to keep the audience engaged. The goal is to offer clarity without overwhelming listeners with unnecessary detail. Speak with intention, using language that is accessible and confident, avoiding technical jargon unless it's essential and well-explained.

Adding examples, statistics, or case studies to your responses can significantly enhance their impact. These supporting elements not only lend authenticity but also help your audience Visualise and relate to your message. For instance, if you're asked about the potential impact of a new policy, citing a relevant statistic or describing a real-world example brings depth and weight to your answer. These concrete details build trust and make your message more persuasive.

Being thoroughly prepared with your answers allows you to handle questions with ease and professionalism. It boosts your confidence and enables you to think clearly under pressure, helping you stay composed even when faced with unexpected or challenging inquiries. Your preparation will be evident, and the audience will appreciate your thoughtful, informed responses.

To make the session more engaging and efficient, it helps to think about how your questions and answers can be organised in advance. Grouping similar questions together—by theme, topic, or level of complexity—can create a more natural, coherent flow. For example, in a presentation on environmental policy, it can be useful to address questions about the economic impact first, then transition to those dealing with legislation or social change. This thoughtful sequencing helps the audience follow along more easily and encourages deeper exploration of related ideas. It also allows you to avoid repeating yourself and to build on earlier answers, gradually reinforcing key messages.

One of the most effective ways to prepare for a real Q&A session is to hold a mock session in advance. Invite colleagues, mentors, or peers to simulate a live audience and ask a range of questions, especially the challenging or unpredictable ones. Practicing in a realistic setting helps sharpen your ability to think on your feet, adapt your messaging, and respond with confidence. These rehearsal sessions not only improve your delivery but also give you valuable insight into how others might interpret your content, helping you refine both your answers and your presentation overall.

Mock Q&A sessions are an invaluable tool for building confidence and preparing for the real event. Begin by inviting colleagues or mentors to create a setting that mimics a live Q&A environment. Encourage them to ask a variety of questions, especially those that challenge your thinking or push you to elaborate further. This will help you think on your feet and practice handling unexpected inquiries with ease.

As you go through these practice sessions, focus on refining your answers. Aim to make your responses clear, concise, and impactful. Pay attention to which answers resonate with your mock audience and which ones may need more refinement. This feedback is crucial—it highlights areas where you can improve and helps you hone your communication skills, ensuring that you're delivering your message in the most effective way possible.

Beyond improving your responses, mock sessions also help you manage nerves or anxiety. Preparing in a safe, supportive environment boosts your confidence, allowing you to become more comfortable in high-pressure situations. Over time, this resilience will carry over into your actual Q&A session, making it feel less daunting and more like an opportunity for meaningful interaction.

By treating these mock sessions as an essential step in your preparation, you'll transform what could be a stressful experience into a rewarding exchange with your audience. When the time comes for your actual Q&A, you will walk into the room feeling prepared, assured, and ready to handle anything that comes your way.

Q&A Preparation Checklist:

1. **Anticipate Questions:** Identify potential inquiries based on your speech and audience interests.

2. **Review Past Presentations:** Note any recurring questions or themes to prepare for similar ones.

3. **Craft Comprehensive Answers:** Develop detailed yet concise responses, backed by examples and data.

4. **Organise by Theme:** Group questions by topic or difficulty to maintain a structured flow.

5. **Engage in Mock Sessions:** Practice with colleagues or mentors to tackle challenging questions and build confidence.

How to Handle Unpredictable Questions

By now, you should feel well-prepared after practicing your mock Q&A session. Facing unexpected questions during a presentation can be daunting, but with the right preparation, you can handle them confidently and with poise. Begin by anticipating the more challenging questions related to your topic. Think about themes that may spark concern or scepticism within your audience. If your subject matter is contentious, be prepared for deeper, more probing questions that seek to explore the controversy. Having well-reasoned responses for different viewpoints not only showcases your expertise but also highlights your openness to engaging in meaningful, thoughtful dialogue.

When challenging questions arise, it's crucial to maintain a steady demeanour and stay calm as you address the issues at hand. Rather than rushing into an answer, take a moment to pause. This brief silence serves two purposes: it allows you to gather your thoughts and signals to the audience that you're carefully considering their question. When you respond, use bridging statements to guide your answer back to your main message. For instance, phrases like "That's an interesting point; let's explore that further" help steer the conversation back on track while acknowledging the concern or curiosity behind the question.

By remaining composed and using thoughtful responses, you not only address difficult questions effectively but also maintain control of the conversation, reinforcing your credibility as a confident and knowledgeable speaker.

It's also important to keep the discussion centred on your main points. If you receive an off-topic question, acknowledge its relevance but redirect the conversation. For example, you could say, "That's an important issue, but it falls outside our discussion today. Let's focus on..." This approach keeps the dialogue anchored in your central themes.

Addressing hostile questioners can be quite difficult, yet it is vital to remain professional. Remember, beneath the surface of hostility often lie deeper issues that need to be addressed. Deal with these underlying issues rather than engaging with the hostility itself. Remain calm, use a steady tone, and respond with honesty. For instance, you might say, "I understand your concern, and here's how I see it..." This not only defuses tension but also allows for a constructive dialogue. By handling confrontational questions with grace, you maintain your credibility and project confidence.

Close Your Q and A Session with Impact

As your Q&A session draws to a close, it's essential to gently guide the conversation back to the central themes of your presentation. This final moment is more than just a wrap-up—it's an opportunity to reinforce the key messages you want your audience to carry with them. By briefly summarizing the most important takeaways, you help solidify your message and bring the discussion full circle. Rather than simply repeating what's already been said, connect your answers back to the overarching narrative of your presentation. Highlight the points that matter most, ensuring your audience leaves with a clear and coherent understanding of your insights and the value you've provided.

This is also the perfect time to clear up any lingering misunderstandings, address any final concerns, and reemphasize the conclusions that support your main argument. When you restate these ideas with intention and clarity, it not only strengthens your position but also leaves a polished, professional impression.

A powerful closing statement is your final chance to make your message resonate. Think of it as the punctuation mark that gives your entire talk meaning and closure. Let it reflect your central ideas, reaffirm the purpose behind your presentation, and offer your audience something to hold onto—whether it's a call to action, a thoughtful takeaway, or a compelling thought that invites deeper reflection. This moment helps you leave a lasting impression, one that continues to echo long after the session ends.

To keep the momentum going, invite your audience to stay connected beyond the session. Share your contact information— email, website, or professional social media handles—and encourage them to reach out with follow-up thoughts or questions. This small gesture speaks volumes. It shows that you value their engagement, welcome their perspectives, and are open to continuing the conversation in a more personal and thoughtful way. It transforms the session from a one-time event into the beginning of an ongoing dialogue

Finally, never underestimate the power of a sincere thank you. Take a moment to express genuine appreciation for your audience's time, attention, and thoughtful participation. Acknowledge their presence and the questions they brought forward—it's their engagement that turns your presentation into a shared experience. By showing gratitude, you not only close on a gracious note but also deepen the connection you've built, leaving your audience feeling valued, respected, and truly heard.

How to Manage Technical Malfunctions on Stage

What do you do when giving a presentation, fully engaged with your audience and suddenly, the microphone cuts out or the projector malfunctions? These technical glitches happen to everyone. Recognising and handling these disruptions quickly is key. They can include anything from a buzzing microphone to a flickering screen, and unexpected announcements can throw you off your game too.

The first step is to stay calm. It's easy to feel flustered, but maintaining composure reflects professionalism and confidence. Try mindful breathing to help you centre yourself. Inhale slowly, hold for a moment, then exhale deeply. This little technique can clear your mind and keep you focused. Your body language is also important—stand tall with relaxed shoulders and make eye contact. This posture not only shows confidence but also reassures your audience that you're in control, even when things get tricky.

When you're ready to get back on track, smooth transitions matter. Use phrases like "Now, as we were discussing" or "Let's return to our main point" to shift your audience's focus back to the topic. A quick recap of what you were discussing before the interruption can also help refresh their memory and keep them engaged.

Interruptions can even be an opportunity to connect more with your audience. Share a relevant story or personal anecdote to fill the gap—this makes your presentation feel more relatable. You could also invite audience participation by asking an interesting question or encouraging them to share their thoughts. Engaging your listeners during these moments strengthens the connection between you and your audience and keeps the energy flowing.

By using these strategies, you'll ensure that your message remains clear and engaging, no matter what disruptions arise.

How to Navigate Audience Reactions?

The ability to read and respond to audience reactions is a subtle yet powerful skill that can elevate your presentation from good to unforgettable. As you step onto the stage and begin sharing your message, your delivery doesn't exist in a vacuum—your audience is constantly providing you with valuable feedback through their body language, facial expressions, and other non-verbal cues. Paying attention to these subtle signals allows you to adapt in real time, creating a more responsive and engaging experience for everyone in the room.

Look closely at how your audience physically responds to your words. A slight lean forward, widened eyes, or a thoughtful nod can indicate that your message is landing well, sparking curiosity or agreement. These are the green lights—signs that your energy is being met with genuine interest. Eye contact and warm, open facial expressions are also strong indicators of connection. They suggest that your ideas are not only being heard but felt.

On the other hand, signs of disengagement or discomfort can emerge just as clearly. If someone begins fidgeting, frequently checks their phone, or appears to be whispering to their neighbour, it may suggest that their attention is drifting. Crossed arms, furrowed brows, or a slouched posture could signal confusion, resistance, or even scepticism. These cues aren't necessarily negative—they're opportunities. Recognising them gives you the chance to re-engage, clarify, or shift your tone to better meet the audience's needs.

Being attuned to these non-verbal messages lets you gauge the emotional temperature of the room and adjust accordingly. You might pause to pose a question, add a relatable story, or emphasize a key point more clearly. The goal isn't to rigidly control every moment, but to remain present and flexible—tuning in to your audience's reactions and responding in ways that deepen the connection.

In doing so, you create a conversation, even when you're the only one speaking. Your sensitivity to the unspoken makes your message more resonant, your delivery more impactful, and your presence more memorable.

In addition to non-verbal cues, listening for verbal feedback is crucial. Sounds of murmurs, laughter, or agreement can deepen your understanding of how your message is being received. By closely monitoring these various forms of feedback, you can adapt your delivery in real-time, making necessary adjustments that help ensure your message resonates effectively with your audience. Through this attentive approach, you can create a more engaging and dynamic speaking experience.

Once you've taken the time to understand your audience's mood and engagement level, it's crucial to adapt your delivery to match their needs. If you start to sense restlessness in the room, consider modifying your pacing. For instance, accelerating your speech can help to rekindle their interest and draw them back into the conversation, while deliberately slowing down your delivery can serve to highlight and underscore key points, allowing your message to resonate more deeply.

If you detect any signs of confusion among your listeners, repeating or rephrasing your main ideas can clarify your message and ensure it is understood.

The use of personal anecdotes and vivid examples significantly enriches your message, ensuring your speech leaves a lasting impression. These compelling stories bring your points to life, fostering a strong connection with your audience. Adaptability is crucial; it cultivates a dynamic environment during your presentation, transforming it into an engaging experience that mirrors a genuine conversation. By actively observing and responding to your audience's body language and expressions, you not only enhance their comprehension but also elevate their overall experience.

When you encounter indifferent or negative reactions, recognise them as valuable opportunities for growth. Acknowledge any discomfort directly; a confident statement like, "I see some of you are deep in thought," validates their feelings and stimulates engagement. Transform negative feedback into a chance to clarify concerns or misconceptions. For instance, if you notice a furrowed brow, take the initiative to elaborate and enhance understanding. Your assertive and receptive demeanour can effectively convert criticism into a productive dialogue, reinforcing your connection with the audience and fostering a truly interactive experience.

On the other hand, when you receive positive reactions, seize those moments to reinforce your message. Smiles, nods, and applause create a golden opportunity to build momentum. Encourage participation by asking open-ended questions or inviting comments. This engagement energizes the room and validates your message, demonstrating its impact. Responding enthusiastically to positive feedback can amplify the excitement, creating a ripple effect. Building on these responses enriches the conversation and strengthens your connection with the audience. This shared experience fosters a sense of community and leaves a lasting impression that resonates well beyond your presentation.

Adopt Improv Skills

Public speaking often comes with surprises, and adapting to these unexpected moments can be both challenging and rewarding. One essential skill for navigating these situations is improvisation, or improv. Improv allows you to create dialogue and actions spontaneously, without a script. This practice boosts your creativity and helps you think on your feet, making it easier to respond naturally and confidently to unexpected questions or comments during a presentation.

To improve your improv skills, consider incorporating specific exercises into your preparation routine. Improv games, like quick-thinking word associations, encourage mental agility and responsiveness. You can do these exercises alone or with others, creating a playful environment where you can experiment without fear of judgment. Another valuable technique is the "Yes, and..." approach. This involves accepting what others say and building on it, rather than contradicting or dismissing their input with "but". Actors actively use this technique to build on one another's actions and suggestions, creating dynamic and powerful scenes that engage the audience. In a public speaking context, acknowledging audience contributions and expanding on them fosters a collaborative atmosphere.

Applying improv skills in real-time can greatly enhance your public speaking experience. For instance, if an audience member shares an unexpected insight during your presentation, use your improv skills to incorporate their input into your narrative. Craft spontaneous stories that connect their contribution to your main points, enriching your message. This not only keeps your audience engaged but also showcases your adaptability and willingness to embrace diverse perspectives.

Cultivating an improv mind-set is about embracing openness and flexibility in your speaking engagements. It encourages you to see challenges as opportunities for growth and connection rather than sticking rigidly to a script. This mind-set creates a dynamic interaction where both you and your audience contribute to the conversation, inviting spontaneity and innovation. With practice, you can develop an improv mind-set that enhances your public speaking and empowers you to handle any situation with confidence and grace.

Overall, the ability to improvise is crucial in public speaking, offering tools for creativity and adaptability. As you embrace these skills, you'll connect with audiences in meaningful and unexpected ways. This chapter has highlighted techniques to improve your adaptability, paving the way for further exploration of dynamic communication strategies. In the next and last chapter, we'll outline a long-term plan for growth and mastery in public speaking, building on the skills you've developed here.

Chapter 12:
Long-Term Growth and Mastery

Public speaking often comes with surprises, and adapting to these unexpected moments can be both challenging and rewarding. One essential skill for navigating these situations is improvisation, or improv. Improv allows you to create dialogue and actions spontaneously, without a script. This practice boosts your creativity and helps you think on your feet, making it easier to respond naturally and confidently to unexpected questions or comments during a presentation.

To improve your improv skills, consider incorporating specific exercises into your preparation routine. Improv games, like quick-thinking word associations, encourage mental agility and responsiveness. You can do these exercises alone or with others, creating a playful environment where you can experiment without fear of judgment. Another valuable technique is the "Yes, and..." approach. This involves accepting what others say and building on it, rather than contradicting or dismissing their input with "but". Actors actively use this technique to build on one another's actions and suggestions, creating dynamic and powerful scenes that engage the audience. In a public speaking context, acknowledging audience contributions and expanding on them fosters a collaborative atmosphere.

Applying improv skills in real-time can greatly enhance your public speaking experience. For instance, if an audience member shares an unexpected insight during your presentation, use your improv skills to incorporate their input into your narrative. Craft spontaneous stories that connect their contribution to your main points, enriching your message. This not only keeps your audience engaged but also showcases your adaptability and willingness to embrace diverse perspectives.

Cultivating an improv mind-set is about embracing openness and flexibility in your speaking engagements. It encourages you to see challenges as opportunities for growth and connection rather than sticking rigidly to a script. This mind-set creates a dynamic interaction where both you and your audience contribute to the conversation, inviting spontaneity and innovation. With practice, you can develop an improv mind-set that enhances your public speaking and empowers you to handle any situation with confidence and grace.

Overall, the ability to improvise is crucial in public speaking, offering tools for creativity and adaptability. As you embrace these skills, you'll connect with audiences in meaningful and unexpected ways. This chapter has highlighted techniques to improve your adaptability, paving the way for further exploration of dynamic communication strategies. In the next and last chapter, we'll outline a long-term plan for growth and mastery in public speaking, building on the skills you've developed here.

Life often places us at important crossroads, each path offering enticing possibilities but only one ultimately leading to our true aspirations. This concept lies at the heart of establishing long-term goals, particularly in the realm of public speaking. As a Reverend Minister, devoted husband, and proud father of three incredible children, I've come to understand that true mastery isn't something you achieve overnight; instead, it unfolds as a continuous journey of growth and self-discovery.

Goals setting is like creating a detailed map for your journey, guiding you through the winding paths and unexpected challenges you may face. Without these essential markers, it's easy to get lost, wandering in circles and missing out on the incredible heights you could achieve. Goals light your way, acting as bright beacons of inspiration during tough times and reminding you of your purpose, especially when the road becomes steep and daunting. By embracing this path with clear, intentional goals, you create a solid foundation for personal growth and fulfillment in your speaking journey. Each step forward becomes a meaningful part of your transformation, leading you closer to the success you envision.

To set effective goals, consider the SMART framework: Specific, Measurable, Achievable, Relevant, and Time-bound. This approach helps you define clear and attainable objectives. For example, if you want to speak at a major conference, break this goal into smaller steps. Identify the conference, note the submission deadlines, and craft a compelling proposal. Set milestones—like completing a draft by a specific date—to track your progress. By focusing on these tangible tasks, you convert a daunting aspiration into a series of manageable objectives, each one bringing you closer to your dream.

Short-term and long-term goals balancing is crucial for sustainable growth. While your long-term goals point you in the right direction, short-term objectives act as stepping stones. Consistent weekly practice can improve your skills gradually, laying the groundwork for larger achievements. Enrol in advanced speaking courses to also enhance your abilities, introducing you to new techniques and insights. By aligning these short-term efforts with your long-term aspirations, you create a cohesive plan for continuous improvement.

As you pursue your goals, be flexible and willing to adapt. Regularly reassess your objectives to ensure they remain relevant and challenging. This might mean reviewing your goals quarterly, checking your progress, and making adjustments as needed. Be open to new opportunities or shifts in your priorities. By combining feedback and reflecting on your journey, you can refine your goals to match your evolving vision. This adaptability allows you to stay on course while embracing new possibilities, keeping your journey dynamic and fulfilling.

Interactive Element: Goal-Setting Template

To effectively organise your objectives, consider using a goal-setting template.

1.   Begin by identifying your long-term goal, such as speaking at an international conference.

2.   Then, break this goal into smaller, manageable tasks, like researching conferences and preparing your submission.

3.   Set deadlines for each task, and make it a habit to review your progress regularly.

This approach will help you stay focused and motivated on your journey, allowing you to celebrate your achievements and adjust your plans as needed. With this structured method, you'll move closer to mastering public speaking.

12.2 Embrace New Opportunities

There is a saying which goes that "opportunity comes but once" when you're about to speak in a venue like no other, this is where you can find new opportunities to enhance your public speaking journey, it is also the time to make a full proof of your speaking talents and abilities.

Consider exploring unconventional venues like art galleries, open-air festivals, or cosy local cafes. These unique settings can captivate audiences that wouldn't typically attend traditional speaking events. They allow you to connect with diverse groups, broadening your reach and improving your adaptability. Additionally, participating in international conferences can elevate your speaking experience by connecting you with global audiences, enriching your understanding of different cultures and perspectives. Engaging with these audiences challenges you to make your message universally relatable.

To venture into the unknown can feel overwhelming, yet embracing new opportunities is crucial for personal growth. One powerful technique to build confidence is Visualisation. See yourself stepping onto the stage, your heart racing with excitement, as you successfully engage your audience and absorb the vibrant energy of the room. This mental rehearsal not only calms your nerves but also cultivates an empowering sense of assurance.

Start by embracing small, intentional steps that help you grow more comfortable with public speaking. Taking manageable risks early on can set the stage for greater opportunities down the road. For instance, consider volunteering at a community event where you can contribute your voice and energy toward a collective goal. These low-pressure environments allow you to interact with others while building a sense of purpose and confidence. Another great option is to participate in a panel discussion—whether in person or virtually—where you can share your perspectives in a collaborative setting. Each of these experiences adds to your skill set, gradually increasing your comfort and readiness for more prominent speaking roles.

As you gather these experiences, your confidence will naturally build, making it easier to step into larger and more influential spaces. Over time, what once felt intimidating will begin to feel like a natural extension of your voice and values.

One of the most effective ways to uncover new speaking opportunities is through networking, a topic explored in depth in Chapter 9. Platforms such as LinkedIn and Twitter are valuable tools for staying connected with professionals in your field and staying informed about upcoming events. Engage actively—join discussions, comment on posts, share your insights, and make your interest in speaking visible. Let your online presence reflect your voice, your message, and your desire to contribute. You never know who might come across your content and think of you for their next event.

In addition to digital spaces, joining professional organisations like Toastmasters International or the National Speakers Association can provide meaningful connections with like-minded individuals. These communities often offer speaking opportunities, training, and mentorship, making them excellent spaces for both learning and exposure. Building genuine relationships within these networks creates a strong foundation for long-term collaboration and growth.

When a speaking opportunity does arise, take time to evaluate it through a thoughtful lens. Ask yourself whether the event aligns with your personal brand and long-term goals. Will participating enhance your credibility, strengthen your reputation, and showcase your expertise in the right light? Also, consider your audience— does your message resonate with them, and can it bring them value? Thinking about these aspects helps ensure that the opportunities you pursue are not only beneficial professionally but also meaningful personally.

Finding the right balance between fulfillment and advancement is what will sustain your passion for public speaking. Let every step—no matter how small—be guided by authenticity and a commitment to growth. The journey isn't about becoming someone else; it's about becoming more of who you already are, and allowing that voice to reach and inspire others.

Reflection Section: Opportunity Assessment

Take a moment to think about the opportunities that have come your way.

1.   Write them down and assess how well each aligns with your brand and audience.

2.   Consider the skills you could gain and the connections you might make.

This reflection will help you choose opportunities that match your long-term goals and support your growth.

12.3 Reflection on Personal Growth

At the end of a long, full day, your mind may be buzzing—thoughts colliding, moments replaying, lessons slowly surfacing. Reflection in public speaking is very much like that pause you take before winding down: a quiet, honest check-in with yourself. It's an opportunity to process what happened, to acknowledge what went well, and to gently notice where there's room to grow. This practice isn't just helpful—it's essential. Reflection becomes the bridge between experience and improvement.

Through regular reflection, you gain clarity about your strengths. Maybe you realise you have a knack for telling stories that captivate, or you're particularly good at breaking down complex concepts into something your audience can understand and relate to. Identifying these strengths provides a solid base—one you can intentionally build upon as you continue developing your speaking style.

But just as importantly, reflection shines a light on the areas that need refinement. Perhaps you noticed your transitions between points felt a bit clunky, or that you struggled to fully engage certain audience members. These are not failures—they're signposts, helping you map out your next steps. When approached with curiosity and compassion, these observations can fuel meaningful progress and growth.

For your reflection to be truly useful, it helps to bring in structure. One powerful habit is keeping a public speaking journal. After each presentation, jot down a few honest reflections: What felt strong? What moments surprised you? Where did you feel in sync, and where did things feel a little off? Over time, this journal becomes more than just a record—it becomes a mirror of your journey, showing how far you've come and what still lies ahead.

You can also incorporate quick self-evaluations after each talk. Take a moment to mentally replay the experience: Were your key points clear? Did you adapt well to audience reactions? Did the room feel connected, or was there something missing in the flow? These kinds of questions sharpen your awareness and help transform reflection from a passive act into a focused tool for growth.

The truth is, improvement doesn't just happen in front of the microphone. It happens in the quiet moments afterward, when you choose to learn from your own experience. That simple pause—honest, consistent, and intentional—is where the real transformation begins.

Balance lessons from both successes and failures to foster growth and when analysing successful speeches, identify strategies you can use again—like a powerful story you opened with or a humorous moment that built rapport. Meanwhile, challenging experiences also offer valuable lessons. For instance, a technical glitch might disrupt your flow, or an unexpected audience question could throw you off. These uncomfortable moments teach resilience, adaptability, and the importance of preparation. By embracing both success and failure, you develop a well-rounded perspective that prepares you for any scenario.

Once you've taken time to reflect, it's important to turn those insights into action. Setting new learning goals based on your reflections is a powerful way to grow as a speaker. These goals might include sharpening your storytelling, improving your use of visual aids, or becoming more comfortable with impromptu speaking. Let your goals stretch you, but also make sure they align with what excites you. When your objectives are both challenging and meaningful, growth feels natural and motivating.

As you pursue these goals, keep your development plan flexible. New strengths will emerge, and fresh opportunities will appear. That's the beauty of continuous learning—it keeps your progress dynamic and evolving. Along the way, explore different speaking styles. If your default is formal and structured, try speaking in a more casual, conversational tone. This kind of variety not only keeps your presentations engaging, but also builds your adaptability.

Reflection is more than just a tool for improvement—it's a chance to pause and appreciate your journey. Every talk you give, every hurdle you overcome, is part of your progress. These moments deserve recognition. They show how far you've come and help you identify where you want to go next.

In the end, reflection is your compass. It helps you navigate your growth with intention, reminding you of your strengths while pointing you toward new opportunities. By staying curious and committed, you empower yourself to speak with confidence, authenticity, and purpose.

12.4 Sustain Mastery through Lifelong Learning

Just as an artist meticulously hones their techniques, blending brushstrokes and experimenting with new hues to bring depth, texture, and emotion to a canvas, the journey of public speaking is a similarly evolving and creative endeavour. Every speech or presentation is an opportunity not only to share ideas but to refine one's voice, captivate an audience, and communicate with clarity, authenticity, and passion. Much like artistry, the mastery of public speaking is not a destination but a continuous process—an ever-unfolding path of growth, exploration, and transformation. Each speaking engagement presents a new challenge, a fresh insight, and a chance to evolve.

One of the most effective ways to accelerate this growth is by enrolling in advanced communication courses. These structured learning environments provide far more than just techniques—they offer fresh frameworks, peer interactions, and feedback loops that self-guided practice often lacks. Such programs are designed to stretch your existing understanding, encouraging you to explore various delivery styles, persuasive strategies, and storytelling approaches. They don't just teach you *how* to speak—they teach you how to speak *with impact*.

Complementing this, workshops and masterclasses offer immersive, often hands-on experiences that allow for direct interaction with seasoned professionals and coaches. These sessions offer immediate, constructive feedback that can illuminate blind spots, fine-tune delivery, and build confidence. The ability to practice, reflect, and receive guidance in real-time can be transformative—helping you sharpen not only your speaking skills but also your self-awareness, presence, and adaptability. Over time, these experiences cultivate the kind of speaker who not only informs but also inspires and resonates deeply with their audience.

To truly thrive, however, one must become a lifelong learner. In today's digital age, an abundance of diverse and accessible learning resources makes this easier than ever. Platforms like Coursera, Demy, and edX offer a wide variety of free and paid courses tailored to different levels of experience and specific aspects of communication—from storytelling and persuasion to vocal delivery and body language. These platforms provide the flexibility to learn at your own pace, making it possible to integrate education seamlessly into your everyday routine.

Moreover, podcasts, webinars, and video series featuring experienced speakers and thought leaders are rich sources of inspiration and current thinking. Listening to these during commutes, workouts, or downtime can offer bite-sized yet powerful learning moments. They help keep your thinking fresh, expose you to different speaking styles, and spark creative ways to enhance your own presentation techniques.

Staying informed about industry trends is not optional—it's essential in the fast-evolving landscape of public speaking. Social platforms like LinkedIn, X (formerly Twitter), and even Clubhouse are excellent for following key voices in the field. Through them, you can access timely updates, discover emerging topics, and engage with a vibrant community of professionals. By participating in discussions, commenting on posts, and sharing your own content, you don't just passively absorb knowledge—you actively shape your identity and presence within the public speaking ecosystem.

Additionally, immersing yourself in dedicated public speaking blogs, newsletters, and industry publications provides a more in-depth understanding of new methodologies and shifting audience expectations. These resources offer case studies, expert analyses, and practical tips that can refine your approach and keep you agile. Whether you're learning how to integrate storytelling into business presentations or how to command attention in virtual meetings, staying current ensures your communication remains relevant and powerful.

Ultimately, becoming a great speaker isn't just about learning to talk well—it's about committing to lifelong curiosity, continual refinement, and the courage to keep showing up. By blending structured learning with informal exploration, feedback with reflection, and passion with persistence, you'll not only improve your speaking ability—you'll transform how you connect with others and how your message lives on in their minds.

Include cutting-edge techniques and advanced technologies into your speaking practice to significantly enhance your communication skills. Explore the use of immersive tools, such as virtual reality and engaging interactive software, to transform your presentations into captivating experiences that resonate with your audience. Adopt creative formats like storytelling, which weaves narratives that draw listeners in, and facilitate interactive discussions that encourage audience participation. By fostering a sense of involvement, you can create a profound connection with your audience, ultimately making your message more memorable and impactful.

As you continue to develop your speaking abilities, remember that lifelong learning is about applying what you've learned to real-life situations. Creating meaningful connections with your audience enriches your life and opens doors to new opportunities. Mastery in public speaking is a journey rather than a destination, and also a process rather an event—one of exploration and discovery. By committing to lifelong learning, you ensure your skills stay relevant, your message resonates, and your impact lasts.

As we conclude in the next chapter, we'll explore the practical aspects of applying these insights and effortlessly integrating new learning into your public speaking practice.

Conclusion

As you stand on the threshold of becoming a more confident and engaging public speaker, pause for a moment and take it all in. This is not just a milestone—it's a powerful testament to your growth, your courage, and your commitment. You've walked through a journey that many begin, but few see through with such dedication. And now, it's time to look back—not with hesitation, but with pride.

We began where most transformations start: in the space of discomfort and uncertainty. Public speaking anxiety is real. It can make your heart race, your palms sweat, and your voice tremble. But instead of letting that fear hold you back, you learned to lean into it. You discovered that nervous energy doesn't have to be a barrier—it can be a gift. With the right tools and mind-set, you turned that energy into fuel. A force that sharpens your focus, amplifies your presence, and enhances your delivery.

You practiced the art of grounding yourself in the moment. Deep breathing exercises became more than just a technique; they became your anchor. Visualising success became your way of painting a future where you stand tall and speak with conviction. Staying present allowed you to shed the weight of past missteps and future worries, and instead, connect deeply with your message and your audience.

From there, you stepped into the blueprint of great communication—speech structure. You explored the power of intention and clarity. You learned that every effective speech has a strong spine: an opening that captures attention, a body that delivers meaningful content, and a conclusion that leaves a lasting impression. Captivating introductions, once intimidating, now flow from you with ease. Impactful conclusions, once an afterthought, have become your moment to shine, to drive home your message with purpose and poise.

You discovered the secret weapon of every memorable speaker: storytelling. You unearthed the stories within yourself—the small moments, the big lessons, the personal insights—and learned how to shape them into narratives that move people. You found that facts may inform, but stories transform. They breathe life into your message and create emotional connections that linger long after your final words.

Body language, too, became part of your vocabulary. You learned that communication is not just about what you say, but how you say it. Your gestures became more purposeful. Your stance more grounded. Your facial expressions more animated and aligned with your tone. You became aware of how the unspoken complements the spoken, reinforcing your message and building trust with your audience.

Then came your voice—your most personal instrument. You learned how to care for it, warm it up, and use it intentionally. Through vocal exercises, you developed strength, clarity, and flexibility. Pitch, tone, and pace became tools in your toolbox, not obstacles. You discovered how to be dynamic and expressive, keeping your listeners engaged. And you realised that silence, used thoughtfully, is not empty space. Strategic pauses became powerful punctuation—moments where your audience could reflect, absorb, and anticipate.

All of these elements—your calm presence, your structured message, your authentic stories, your expressive body language, your resonant voice—now work together in harmony. They create a complete, compelling version of you as a speaker. A version that is confident, credible, and deeply engaging.

Engaging your audience became an art form we practiced diligently. By researching their interests and tailoring your content, you connected with them through stories and humour. We tackled time management together, ensuring your message was both concise and resonant. With thorough research and persuasive arguments, your confidence grew, allowing you to speak with authority.

Technology became your ally, helping you create seamless presentations and navigate technical challenges effortlessly. We also focused on cultural sensitivity, equipping you to adapt your message for diverse audiences and foster inclusivity. Networking opened new doors for you, as you embraced practice and feedback, transforming unexpected hurdles into valuable lessons.

The key takeaways from our journey go beyond mere strategies— they are life skills. Mastering public speaking can turn you into a confident communicator who leaves a lasting impression. The abilities you've developed extend beyond the stage, enriching your personal and professional life.

Take a moment to appreciate how far you've come. Each step has helped you break down barriers and uncover your full potential. Remember, public speaking is a lifelong journey, not a final destination. Embrace every chance to refine your skills, knowing your efforts will yield incredible rewards.

Now is the perfect time to take action. Seek out opportunities to practice and enhance your abilities. Join local speaking clubs or online groups to connect with fellow speakers. Share your experiences, learn from one another, and become part of a supportive community. Every engagement will boost your confidence and broaden your perspective.

As you master public speaking, countless doors will open—leading to career growth, personal fulfillment, and improved communication. The success you can achieve and the positive changes you can instigate through effective communication are beyond imagination. Your voice has the power to inspire, influence, and drive change.

Thank you for embarking on this journey with me. Your dedication to improving your public speaking skills is commendable, and I'm grateful for your trust in this process. As you continue to grow, remember that every step brings you closer to unlocking your true potential.

To support your continued growth, this guide offers more than just information—it provides a path forward. At the end of each chapter, you'll find practical exercises and actionable steps designed to help you turn knowledge into lasting skill. These aren't just activities—they're opportunities. Opportunities to step out of your comfort zone, to push past your perceived limits, and to track your evolution as a speaker.

Each checklist is a roadmap. Each action item, a stepping stone. Each self-assessment tool, a mirror reflecting how far you've come and where you still wish to go. When used consistently, these tools become more than learning aids—they become trusted companions on your journey, helping you stay aligned, accountable, and inspired.

And now, as we draw this chapter to a close, remember this: mastery is not a destination—it's a practice. Public speaking isn't something you perfect once and leave behind. It's a dynamic, evolving skill—one that grows stronger every time you use it. With dedication, consistency, and an open heart, you will become the engaging, persuasive, and impactful communicator you've envisioned.

Let this not be the end of your progress, but the beginning of a new chapter—one filled with courage, growth, and opportunities to make your voice truly heard. Embrace every challenge that comes your way. Celebrate the small wins. Learn from the setbacks. Each experience adds a new layer of depth to your ability to connect, inspire, and lead through words.

And just so you know—you are not alone. Even after more than 20 years of public speaking, I still feel the flutter of nerves before standing in front of a new and bigger audience. That feeling doesn't mean you're unprepared. It means you care. But here's the truth: the techniques we've explored together—mindful breathing, powerful storytelling, strategic structure, vocal control, authentic engagement—they've never failed me. And they won't fail you either.

So when that inner voice of doubt tries to sneak in, remember this:

"It's not over until you win. It's not over until you overcome."

You will rise.

You will inspire.

You will overcome.

Because you are becoming the remarkable public speaker you were always meant to be.

References

1. 10 Effective Articulation Exercises to Improve Your Speech
   https://www.tajucoaching.com/blog/articulation-exercises-to-improve-speech-clarity
2. 10 Speaker Engagement Strategies for Virtual Events
   https://www.beaconlive.com/blog/10-proven-virtual-event-speaker-engagement-strategies-to-captivate-your-audience-beaconlive
3. 11 SMART Goals Examples for Your Public Speaking Skills
   https://www.developgoodhabits.com/smart-goals-public-speaking/
4. 15 Networking Tips That Land You Speaking Gigs
   https://speakers.success.com/15-networking-tips-that-land-you-speaking-gigs/
5. 20 of the Best Social Media Analytics Tools for Marketers
   https://sproutsocial.com/insights/social-media-analytics-tools/
6. 5 Best Speech Practices From Sir Winston Churchill
   https://www.forbes.com/sites/jerryweissman/2018/04/06/5-best-speech-practices-from-sir-winston-churchill/
7. 8 Elements of Confident Body Language
   https://virtualspeech.com/blog/8-elements-of-confident-body-language
8. 9 Speaking Industry Trends to Watch in 2023
   https://thespeakerlab.com/blog/9-speaking-industry-trends-to-watch-in-2023/
9. 9 Speaking Industry Trends to Watch in 2023
   https://thespeakerlab.com/blog/9-speaking-industry-trends-to-watch-in-2023/
10. Audience Analysis - Communication - University of Pittsburgh
    https://www.comm.pitt.edu/oral-comm-lab/audience-analysis

11. CBT Techniques: Tools for Cognitive Behavioural Therapy
    https://www.healthline.com/health/cbt-techniques
12. Credibility Statements & Speaker Credibility | Types &
    Examples
    https://study.com/academy/lesson/building-credibility-to-persuade.html
13. Cultural Sensitivity - (Intro to Public Speaking) - Fiveable
    https://library.fiveable.me/key-terms/introduction-public-speaking/cultural-sensitivity
14. Diaphragmatic Breathing: The First Step to a Good Voice
    https://umc.edu/Healthcare/ENT/Patient-Handouts/Adult/Speech-Language-Pathology/Voice/Diaphragmatic-Breathing.html
15. Ethos, Pathos, Logos: 3 Pillars of Public Speaking And
    Persuasion - Oratory Club
    https://oratoryclub.com/pillars-of-public-speaking/
16. Exercises to Warm up Your Voice Before a Speech
    https://virtualspeech.com/blog/exercises-warm-up-voice-before-speech
17. Fear of Public Speaking: How Can I Overcome It?
    https://www.mayoclinic.org/diseases-conditions/specific-phobias/expert-answers/fear-of-public-speaking/faq-20058416
18. Handling Interruptions in Public Speaking | by Moiena
    https://medium.com/@serenityscribe/handling-interruptions-in-public-speaking-8f9b9b37d453
19. How Imagery and Visualisation Can Improve Athletic
    Performance
    https://www.verywellfit.com/Visualisation-techniques-for-athletes-3119438
20. How Improv Can Improve Your Public Speaking Skills -
    Microsoft
    https://www.microsoft.com/en-us/microsoft-365-life-hacks/presentations/improv-to-improve-public-speaking-skills

21. How to Create an Impactful Personal Brand Statement https://thespeakerlab.com/blog/creating-an-impactful-personal-brand-statement/
22. How to Hook Your Audience with an Effective Opening https://www.genardmethod.com/blog/how-to-hook-your-audience-with-an-effective-opening
23. How to Manage Your Time More Effectively https://ed.ted.com/lessons/how-to-manage-your-time-more-effectively-according-to-machines-brian-christian
24. How to Survive Q & A https://www.genardmethod.com/blog/bid/130145/how-to-survive-qa
25. How to Use Feedback to Improve Your Public Speaking Skills https://epiphanycoaching.co.uk/2024/08/23/how-to-use-feedback-to-improve-public-speaking-skills/
26. Inclusive Language | Public Speaking https://courses.lumenlearning.com/wm-publicspeaking/chapter/inclusive-language/
27. Inside Amy Cuddy's TED Talk: Summary and the Debate https://www.speeko.co/blog/summary-ted-talk-amy-cuddy-power-poses
28. Les Brown, *It's Not Over Until You Win* (Simon & Schuster, 1998)
29. Non-Verbal Communication Across Cultures https://www.psychologytoday.com/us/blog/between-cultures/201706/non-verbal-communication-across-cultures
30. Online Timer Tool https://www.wp4toastmasters.com/knowledge-base/online-timer-tool/
31. Pauses in a Speech: Why, When and How https://mannerofspeaking.org/2019/11/12/pauses-in-a-speech-why-when-and-how/
32. Public Speakers' Guide to Networking Events https://www.linkedin.com/advice/3/what-do-you-youre-public-speaker-looking-best-networking-j421e

33. Reading Your Audience
https://www.instituteofpublicspeaking.com/reading-your-audience/
34. Real-Time Speech Analytics: A Guide for Contact Centres
https://www.observe.ai/blog/real-time-speech-analytics
35. Speaking to Diverse Audiences
https://www.toastmasters.org/resources/public-speaking-tips/speaking-to-diverse-audiences
36. Tailor Your Speeches for Global Impact - LinguaLinkDC
https://www.lingualinkdc.net/blog/speeches-impact
37. Technical Issues During Sessions: What Can Happen
https://sessionize.com/playbook/technical-issues-during-sessions
38. The Art of Storytelling in Public Speaking
https://voiceplace.com/art-storytelling-public-speaking/
39. The Art of Storytelling in Speeches
https://www.prezent.ai/zenpedia/art-of-storytelling-in-speeches
40. The Best Presentation Software
https://www.pcmag.com/picks/the-best-presentation-software
41. Thought Leadership 101: Building Your Brand Beyond The Stage
https://speakerflow.com/thought-leadership-101-building-your-brand-beyond-the-stage/
42. Time Management: 12 Tips for Your Next Presentation
https://mannerofspeaking.org/2012/01/22/speakers-its-about-time-and-how-to-manage-it/
43. Toastmasters International - Find a Club
https://www.toastmasters.org/find-a-club
44. Top VR Training Programs for Public Speaking Mastery
https://www.linkedin.com/advice/3/what-best-virtual-reality-training-programs-improving-f0oac
45. Using Humour in a Presentation – It's No Laughing Matter
https://www.presentation-guru.com/using-humour-in-a-presentation-its-no-laughing-matter/

46. Using Rhetorical Strategies for Persuasion - Purdue OWL
https://owl.purdue.edu/owl/general_writing/academic_writi
ng/establishing_arguments/rhetorical_strategies.html
47. Visual Aids | Department of Communication
https://www.comm.pitt.edu/visual-aids
48. Vocal Variety: How to Use Tone, Pitch, and Pace for
Impact
https://robinkermode.com/blog/vocal-variety-how-to-use-
tone-pitch-and-pace-for-impact/
49. Why These Speeches Spread—And How Yours Can Too
https://www.heroicpublicspeaking.com/articles/why-these-
speeches-spread
50. Zotero Research Management Software - Library Guides
https://libguides.wwu.edu/zotero

www.ingramcontent.com/pod-product-compliance
Lightning Source LLC
Chambersburg PA
CBHW071402120626
46546CB00002B/784